HOW NOT TO BE LONELY
AT THE TOP

PHILIPPE MATHIJS

PASSIONPRENEUR®
PUBLISHING

HOW NOT TO BE LONELY AT THE TOP

Practical Wisdom for Positive
Corporate Leadership and
High-Performing Teams

PHILIPPE MATHIJS

PASSIONPRENEUR®
PUBLISHING

Publishing information
Publishing and design facilitated by Passionpreneur Publishing
A division of Passionpreneur Organization Pty Ltd
ABN: 48640637529

Melbourne, VIC | Australia
www.passionpreneurpublishing.com

TABLE OF CONTENTS

TESTIMONIALS

"Through your career, no doubt you will be aspiring to a leadership role and what no-one tells you is that often you go in with little preparation or guidance from others. This is the book that I wish I had read back then, and it will serve you well in navigating that exciting part of your career journey. It will also make you realise that you are surrounded by people whom your greatest role will be to develop and coach to go on and be their best selves. This book will also help with that part too."

—CHERYL HINTON,
CHIEF TECHNOLOGY OFFICER

"Philippe offers invaluable, and practical, insights into one of the most challenging aspects of leadership … managing people. Highly recommended tool if you want to build motivated teams with a strong sense of belonging."

—MOUSTAFA HAMWI,
CEO, PASSIONPRENEUR PUBLISHING

"A brilliant reveal of all the things you learn as a leader, but no-one tells you before you get there. A must read for anyone who wants to lead one day plus those who've already found out how lonely it can be at the top."

—TONY EVANS
AUTHOR, FACEBOOK AND META VETERAN,
MARKETING SCIENTIST, AND BUSINESS PSYCHOLOGIST.

Thank you to the senior figures who provided me with such kind words.

To all the people who woke up one day with a new role of managing people and wondered, "How am I going to do this?", I hope this book gives you some hints that will help you in your new world.

ACKNOWLEDGEMENTS

To my incredible wife who pushed me for so long – and never lost patience whilst I was mulling over the idea to write this book. Know that I wouldn't have been able to do it without you. This book would not have been possible without your understanding during late nights, your inspiration during moments of doubt, and your unique Punjabi love embrace when I needed it most.

To my family, for their constant support and letting me be who I am today. As they said to me so many times over the years, "If it was easy, everyone would do it!".

To BK and Weebs and James for being continuously amazing and being themselves.

To the next generation – Arran, Millie and Maisie – in the hope this inspires you.

To Clare, for her humour, tips on making this manuscript come to life and extreme patience as this was my first "baby" … but it definitely won't be the last!

To all of those who believed in me, thank you from the bottom of my heart.

And last, but by no means least, to Moustafa for creating Passionpreneur and having such an amazing group of authors who helped me along the way.

INTRODUCTION

Here is my leadership recipe ... feel free to add your ingredients and personal twists to make it yours!

At the end of his Presidency, US President Barack Obama awarded Joe Biden the Presidential Medal of Freedom. Joe Biden's words really struck me: "... Mr President ... I get to give you advice, I get to be the last guy in the room ... but I get to walk out and you make the decision". For me, this represents the epitome of "being lonely at the top" and what leadership is truly about: making the decision.

I remember my first position of authority after being an individual contributor – that is, someone who doesn't have any people management as part of their job description. After the euphoria settled, it dawned on me that, whilst I had thought it was easy and I knew what to do, I was actually not prepared at all for the world that awaited me. Forward to 2008, when I moved from a small team to running multiple departments on a global scale, and you can begin to understand the "Oh gosh, how am I going to do this!" feeling. Having gained my share of scars, I wanted to share some of the traps I fell into, so you don't need to.

Having spent three decades navigating the intricate web of boardrooms, negotiations, and strategic planning, I've come to realise that loneliness at the summit isn't inevitable. This book serves as a beacon of hope and guidance for those who aspire to lead with confidence, compassion, and resilience. Each chapter in this book explores a specific corporate scenario, drawing upon my wealth of practical experience to offer insights, strategies, and solutions that will help you forge meaningful connections, build a support network, and ultimately ensure that when you're enjoying the view from the top, you're not alone.

Does this mean you're not enough or in the wrong job because you can't figure it all out on your own? ABSOLUTELY NOT! I've been privileged to coach hundreds of clients and executives from many industries and countries who have faced what you might be facing, so trust me when I say you're not alone, and it's not just you who gets overwhelmed and might not initially know what to do or how to do it.

There are many ways to read this book: You can read it like a novel, from beginning to end; or you can read specific chapters that you feel are most relevant to you. Imagine I'm giving you my recipe book for the outstanding chef that you are. It's down to you to add your own twists to make it YOUR recipe. The simple fact you bought this book and are reading it to either improve yourself or to just get another opinion makes you a worthy leader, and one who's looking after their own self-development. No matter if you're a new leader or some-one who's been there for decades, this book was created with you in mind.

I truly hope you enjoy the book, but also have fun reading it. As Oscar Wilde said, "Life is too short to be taken seriously" – and if you feel like getting in touch and sharing what you liked (or didn't like), I'd love that!

Happy reading!

CHAPTER 1

WHAT THEY DON'T TEACH YOU AT SCHOOL

... BUT YOU REALLY NEED TO KNOW.

I've often heard it joked that you don't learn the things you really need to know in school. We arrive at graduation day fully educated, but utterly clueless about how to do our taxes, pack the car for a long drive, check the oil, or unclog a drain when the shower backs up. That's in our personal lives! I discovered that it's the same when you land your first executive role. Those who have been in theirs for a long time might make it look easy, but they don't often warn you of the pitfalls they faced along the way.

I've been an executive for decades now and let me tell you, I've had some interesting moments along the way! As I think about the legacy I want to leave, something is on my mind: I want to share some of my hard-won lessons with you in the hope that it makes you a better executive, that you avoid some of my failures, and ultimately that your people are happier. Many of my moments along the way were great; some of them were less great. For example, I moved up the ranks really quickly in my career, but I was never prepared for the challenges I'd face. One of the challenges happened over-night, and I suddenly became my boss's boss. The instant shift in reporting lines had nothing on the shift in the inter-personal dynamics I felt in those early weeks and months.

One of the first challenges I met was that of being the bad-news messenger. I didn't know how to deal with delivering large amounts of bad news to masses of people, as there was no-one there to guide or mentor me, or to act as a sounding board. I had to do this awful task so often that I was chris-tened *The Hatchet*. Imagine what that loving "nickname" does to your confidence!

And your loneliness.

I started a coaching and training business without thinking about the support I would need. Being a solo professional to start off with is extremely lonely. How did I go about it? I wish there was a book of instructions or a magic wand or a little tooth fairy that could sprinkle powder and make it all better. But the truth is, at first for me there was nothing, just a sheer weight of decisions that needed to be made. And school doesn't tell you how to make them.

LEARNING WHAT SCHOOL DIDN'T TEACH YOU

The good news is, as time went by, there was a series of les-sons I learned along the way. Lessons that helped me connect with people in a positive way as I lived through difficult times. At first, I didn't have the solutions. I learned by making mistakes. I learned by observation, but I learned. Most of the time, without even realising it, those lessons were moulding me and defining me as a leader. They were forging the core of what would define me (namely serving and nurturing people who work for/with me) and how I'd choose to impact people. Imagine my shock when, many years later, people would look at me as someone inspirational … but let's go back to the beginning.

One thing that's really important to me is to listen to and be there for others, especially during challenging times at work. The moment of epiphany for me arose when many people turned to me for guidance, insight, and mentoring because they didn't have the answers, or they felt the pressures put upon them. This was a personal turning point when I realised that as people move up the ranks, they'll feel alone because they don't know who to turn to.

Over the course of my career, I've had many "aha moments". These really made a big difference to me. School gives you theory but doesn't prepare you for work and success. The most important things about managing people aren't taught. You have to learn them as you go along, and you often learn through making errors. School can be amazing for making you the most technical person you can be. During my career, I've been privileged enough to work with incredible people who are engineers, developers, coders, you name it, because they learned all that at school. At best, some of the schools you've attended have taught you some management theories.

But one thing schools have *never* taught anyone I've ever met to date is how to manage people, to interact with them, and to get the best out of them. How to prepare yourself to have that difficult discussion. How to prepare yourself when someone looks at you and says, "What's your strategy? What's your vision?". Because one thing I've learned over time is that when someone asks you, "What's your vision?", you don't have time to prepare for it, and they don't warn you, "Next meeting, I'm going to ask you what your vision is". Sometimes, it's not even the big question, but something as simple as asking you: "What should we do?".

Another key thing I learned over time – and believe me, it was really hard at first – is that using a coach, mentor, or therapist doesn't make you weak or less adequate. In my eyes, it's a sign of strength to know what you're strong at and what you're not.

WE DON'T HAVE TO BE LONELY AT THE TOP

There are lots of things that can come at you when you first land an executive position: the pressure, the expectations, the unspoken things we just inherit along the way. One of them is that if you're at the top, if you're the boss, you're alone. That's why I look back and remember this story fondly: the first time I fessed up and said I needed help.

We were doing a cooking competition as a team-building exercise, where we were put into teams and asked to cook a three-course meal. I was in charge of the main course and my fellow colleagues were in charge of the other parts. At some point, I realised there was no way I could complete all the tasks I had to do in the allotted time, while some of my teammates had nearly finished.

This was the first time I said, "Guys, can you help me? This isn't going to work". The irony (or good news) is that we won the competition and delivered the best meal. When asked what made us win, my colleagues all chipped in and said, "He asked for help. If he didn't, we wouldn't have known what to do and we wouldn't have worked even more closely as a team".

The moral of that story is: You don't have to be on your own. Asking for help will make you really strong, while going it alone will weaken you. And if the company or the person you work for hints that asking for help makes you weak, I'd suggest changing companies.

I've also experienced extreme burnout and pressure where I couldn't handle it all. I was once woken up at 11:30 at night by my boss – we were in the middle of a merger of two companies, and he asked me to randomly pick people from a list to make them redundant. Nothing prepares you for what happens to you at the specific point in time when you know you're about to change people's lives with the snap of your fingers, even when you don't know them and lack the data to make an informed decision.

During a Tony Robbins event, I realised I could change my life by focusing on serving rather than doing. And what it showed me was that the more I focused on myself, the fewer solutions I had. The minute I started focusing on how I can improve this, help others, and encourage people to grow, my life totally changed … and it changed for the better. Paradoxically, the more I started helping people, the more I started helping *myself* – because it showed me that I wasn't the only one facing those challenges.

However, if you're expecting Tony Robbins–style advice from me, you won't get it. In many ways, I'm the exact opposite. When I started applying some of those ideas, changes started happening in my own life and things became very different. I started to feel more in tune with what I needed for myself, as well as for others.

I've been managing teams for nearly thirty years. And for the majority of that time, I've been in executive leadership. I've also been coaching executives for around a decade, which truly changed my perspective. Throughout my career, I've also developed a reputation as someone who can handle the most difficult situations, which I've done across multiple countries and multiple cultures. And it wasn't easy. It was a step-by-step journey, made up of key decisions and choices. We're going to explore some of these further on, including how I opted to run meetings and how I chose to empower people.

I'm not professing that I have all the answers, or that this book is a Bible. But what I'm sharing is my wisdom and how it helped me be who I am today. More than success in numbers, I pride myself on this knowledge. I've given people the worst news of their lives, sat with them as they processed it, and heard them say, "Thank you. This is an opportunity".

In coaching, well over 95% of my clients will tell me at some point, "You've changed my life". Whilst I really coach to help, I *don't* coach to change a life. For me, changing lives happened to be a byproduct of what happens to each person. This book is not about me; it's all about helping people realise they don't have to be on their own when facing tough times or making hard decisions, as well as about how to manage people.

WE ALL NEED PRACTICAL WISDOM

Because school doesn't teach you this, I wanted to give you some of my practical wisdom to help you in this situation. If we don't create a support mechanism and focus on our needs, the higher we climb up the ladder, the heavier the burden and the greater the pressures become.

What made me successful is the fact that I've been there and gained many scars over my thirty-year career. I've run teams from all over the world, from many cultures. And yes, this did lead me to become a coach, then create a coaching school. I passionately want to create a positive ripple in the world and in individual people's lives.

My book helps emerging corporate leaders who are aspiring to manage well and lead others in an inspirational and empowering way. I share actionable insights from years of coaching and elite corporate success so they can create better teams with safe, motivated employees with a strong sense of belonging.

Let's get into it.

CHAPTER 2

NOW YOU'RE MANAGING PEOPLE ... WHAT'S NEXT?

... WHAT GOT ME THERE AND WHAT I'VE LEARNED SINCE THEN.

C ongratulations. You've got your first leadership position, your first management job, and now you *really* need to learn everything you need to know. You've just moved from being an individual contributor to a person who's leading and managing people; this could be your first time as a team leader, your first head of department position where you're managing a bigger team, or even your first C-suite role where you're managing hundreds of people.

By the end of the chapter, you're going to realise that leadership is a brand-new world, but it doesn't have to be an alien planet. In this chapter, you'll get a bird's-eye view of the tools that will enable you to be a successful leader.

I was an individual contributor for quite a while. I was good at it, commanding respect of clients thanks to my deep technical knowledge. Literally overnight, after an amazing performance appraisal, I was told, "Congratulations, we're giving you Team X to manage; you're doing amazing work, and we need a good manager". I still remember my naivety when I said, "Sure, I'd love to" before I even realised that some people in the new team I had to manage were older than me, had tons more experience, and would wonder who that "wet-behind-the-ears kid" was and how he was going to manage them. In my view, what makes corporate life ironic is that, if you don't manage a team (and try to grow it into an empire), then you "haven't succeeded". I wish my then-manager had given me *Managing People* so I could read it and know what I was letting myself into.

Something I've seen in every job I've had is that people expect that the skills you've learned at school or university will be enough for you to manage people. And you're supposed to know how to have a difficult conversation, think strategically, manage a difficult person, motivate a team, and set key performance indicators (KPIs). But guess what? There isn't a recipe book on how to do it. So how are you going to make sure that your promotion is a success rather than a disaster? The higher you go in leadership, the lower your ego has to be.

By that, I mean you've obviously done *something* right, because you've just got that promotion. When you're at school, whether it's technical like engineering or computer science, they've taught you a whole set of skills that have helped make you the person they want to promote. Yet now you're managing people, you realise that your old ways won't work in this new context – so what are you going to do?

When you start managing people, you need to think more externally than internally, and the needs of the people you're leading need to be much more important than yours. In this book, I want to show you how to succeed and how to make it fun ... but a different kind of fun.

What's made me successful at my job was that I genuinely couldn't care less about timelines. All I care about is the people. I see my job as putting them forward and helping them remove roadblocks. That's all I do. If I was given $1 for every time I was told, "You're too nice, your people are going to take advantage of you", or – and this is one of my favourites of all time – "You need to show them you're the boss quickly and make them fear you", I'd probably have a fortune up there with the likes of Elon Musk. In all the teams I've ever built in my career, made up of people much more successful and brighter than I am, my job is to be the roadblock remover, if there's such a thing. The ability to spot the roadblocks and remove them comes from personal experience, but also from the attitude of humility and service that has to come from within you.

LEADING AND MANAGING ARE DIFFERENT

I lead. I don't manage. This might sound pedantic, but there's a huge difference between the two words. Management is all about having a set of tasks to do and working out how the team moves from Task A to Task B to Task C, making sure they complete each task on time. Leading is really creating "followership" within the people. A great leader's people will follow them to the battlefield without asking any questions, no matter what they're asked.

It took me years to understand the deep difference between leadership and management. While it's easy to understand intellectually, it takes much longer for it to truly sink in. I was given massive teams when I very young, and was beyond keen to prove myself by being the most driven (read: the person who overdelivered). I knew how to manage, as that's easy, but *leading* is a very different ball game. In the process of becoming what I thought was a great leader (which really was an over-keen manager), I'd lost some of my humanity.

LEADERS ARE HUMAN

Emerging leaders are human – believe it or not – and, as a leader, you'll make mistakes. So my tip is, go and make the mistakes, then learn from them. My job as a leader is to make sure that the sandpit you play in is small enough that your mistakes won't cost the company millions, but big enough that you *do* make mistakes. The antithesis of this is quite interesting, as it happened to me when I had what I like to refer to as the "Midas touch". For a period of my career, I grew very fast, getting promoted/headhunted many times. Each time, I had a bigger role, more responsibilities, a tougher target, and an "impossible project" to fix. During those times, I would fearlessly push myself and my teams further and faster; to be fair, we gained major kudos from very senior management. What I *didn't* notice, though, is the personal transformation I was going through: I was expecting everything and everyone in my life to jump when I asked them to and for things to happen "yesterday". Looking back, I see that my rapid success de-humanised me. Thankfully, age and experience gave me wisdom, and some costly mistakes brought me back down to earth as they allowed me to learn from them, then put them into the "never to be repeated" box.

SOFT SKILLS – THE KEY TO GOOD LEADERSHIP

For me, soft skills are crucial to good leadership. As an example, praise in public and chastise in private. I've seen examples of that being done the other way around, and the disastrous effect it has on a company. I've seen people all the way to the most senior position decide that, because Person A and Person B did something wrong, it was a great idea to tell them off in public, sometime in an extremely brutal way. The effect was always the same. The person on the receiving end felt like they were back in kindergarten, their confidence got destroyed, and (funnily enough) they left the company soon after. So don't make that mistake.

For me, having a one-on-one conversation behind closed doors is the place to explain to people why something isn't working well; but in public, my job is to stand by and support them (even if they're wrong). And when they've got it right, one of my favourite things is to really talk them up – so much so that they might even blush and think, "Wow, I didn't realise I'd done such a good job".

How did I see the difference between leaders and managers and individual contributors?

I've been privileged enough in my career to work with several insanely talented people, including some from Ivy League universities or with PhDs, and they all have one thing in common: They were skilled enough to do things like put a rocket on the moon, because their insights are incredible.

On the other hand, they lacked the language to present their insights to upper management. At the beginning of my career, I was working with people who could write the codes needed to put a rocket on the moon in an afternoon. When asked to present the code to more senior people, however, they couldn't articulate it. The point is, some of those people failed in their jobs and were seen as underperformers when they weren't – we just needed to apply different thinking.

The reason is that the language they needed to know was different to the language they spoke. To help those people, I taught them a new language step by step, which completely changed the way they think. It allowed them to change the way they see data and the information they use, while giving their words more of a business twist so upper management could understand them.

In the following chapters, we're going to go through different approaches and answers to tough questions. For example, **Are you wired like a chief operating officer (COO) or chief executive officer (CEO)?** In that chapter (Chapter 3), we're going to see that everyone has different wiring. The brain works in different ways ... the beauty is that no-one is right or wrong. It's all about how we embrace those differences and use everyone's strengths to arrive at the result **AND** give a profound sense of satisfaction to all the people who helped.

A chapter that's close to my heart is *Are you too quiet, too nice, or too anything?* This is because so many times during my career, I've been told things like: "Ah, you're too quiet, or too nice, or too x, or too y, or not enough z". In that chapter (Chapter 4), we're going to look at the perceptions people have of you and how that affects you. And we're going to use that to *really* start understanding more about who you are, what your traits and behaviours are, and what makes you tick. We'll cover what's important to you and what's less important to you, and how we deal with that.

Once we've got the foundation, we're going to move on to **Are you visible enough?** This chapter (Chapter 5) is all about branding. In my coaching experience, many people tell me that they don't need a personal brand, but they want to be promoted – yet that's not happening. What's going on? The point about branding and visibility is finding out how to make sure you have the best brand for what you want to do. And funnily enough, branding is like clothing – just as you don't wear the same clothes every day, you should have different brands for different things you do.

Then we're going to move on to one of the leadership areas that I've seen work brilliantly when done well – or can make people cringe within seconds when done badly. In Chapter 6, it's all about finding out **how you command the room without taking it over.** We've all been in meetings where one person comes in, barks at the room, makes people cringe … and then usually departs, leaving people wondering what just happened. We're going to see how to do the *exact opposite* of that. How can you be that person who leads the room and motivates others to help you solve the problem you're trying to fix?

We're also going to talk about **tough conversations** (Chapter 7). I wanted to talk about this issue, as it's my biggest challenge. The hardest conversation I've ever had to have is one where I say, "Well, we're going to part ways". What does that mean? How do you prepare for that? How do you prepare the other person? We're going to explore different tips and techniques, so you know what to expect from those conversations.

Moving on from tough conversations, in Chapter 8 we're going to look at something much more fun – **how to be inspirational.** What does that mean? Are you born inspirational, or is it something you learn? How do you read that magic moment where someone calls you inspirational for the first time in your career, and you realise ... "Wow, I really *am* inspirational!"?

Then, in Chapter 9, we'll cover what to do when **you've made it to executive level** – an amazing achievement which you should proudly pat yourself on the back for. But so what? What does that mean? What happens next? What's the difference between leading a team, leading two teams, three teams, to executive level where you lead the whole department (or even the company at times)?

Chapter 10 is close to my heart because I've been there: **How do you manage burnout?** What's burnout? What does that mean? I wanted to share with you some of my personal tips on how to manage it and how not to overcommit ... So in a nutshell, this book will help to start learning what they don't teach you at school.

CHAPTER 3

ARE YOU WIRED LIKE A COO OR A CEO?

... AND WHY IT MATTERS FOR YOUR DAY-TO-DAY HAPPINESS.

I've often mused about whether the COO and CEO positions are destined to forever be like cats and dogs, or whether there's a way that both can coexist in something like harmony. Do you feel like pulling your hair out when your boss or colleague comes to you with their ideas? Are you dreading what is, in your mind, a two-minute big-picture conversation that could end up being a thirty-minute to an infinitely-small-level-of-details chat?

A while (OK, a long while) ago, I was managing clients who were very business-oriented and had an ambitious expansion target for their business. The software we were developing was crucial for them, especially one of the modules about customer billing. Talking to one of the people who was helping write the code, I was conveying some customer feedback regarding a feature they saw as important. What I *didn't* expect was the next thirty minutes of my life to be taken up with the person explaining intricate details of their job, while all I wanted to know was whether it was possible or not. Does this mean they were wrong in the way they explained things, and I was right? No! This was the first time I realised we spoke totally different languages, even though we both expressed ourselves in English.

By the end of this chapter, you'll discover your internal wiring and what it means. You'll also learn how other people are wired – and why being different from you doesn't make them the enemy. Why? Because when we know how we're wired, and how *others* are wired, we can learn to navigate our shared terrain.

Have you ever been in a situation where you wondered, "What planet is my boss on?" or "Are we even speaking the same language? I have no idea what they're trying to say!"? If the answer's yes, you're not alone. I've experienced many occasions where a CEO I was working for came up with an idea as strange as, "Let's go to Mars by next week". All I could think of in response was, "But we haven't even invented the aeroplane. How can we travel to Mars, especially so soon?".

I was once working for a company that decided to go paper-less within a year. Technologically, this was very easy. We just needed to apply a few servers, and the IT job was done. Yet the CEO had forgotten that pushing out a new project isn't about the *technology* – it's about changing the mindset. His thought process was: "This is my idea; it sounds great". And to be fair, it *was* the right thing for the company. Let's just sprinkle some pixie dust to make it happen, then the company will be paperless. Unfortunately, it doesn't work that easily. How can we as a company change the mindsets of different people who are wired differently? Even more fundamentally, how can we speak their language to help them accept the change?

What's the secret sauce? What's the magic recipe? First, we'll identify whether you're wired like a CEO or COO. (If you're new in your job, it really *is* the concept that matters.) To help you, I've created a questionnaire (which you'll find in Appendix 1).

To create a big picture, draw a brain on a piece of paper and imagine that the front of your head (where your eyes are) is on the top. Divide it in four to create quadrants.

Chairman

4th Quadrant:
Expand on ideas
Reinvention

1st Quadrant:
Dreamers/Experimentors
Ideas

Board of directors

2nd Quadrant:
Predictability/Process

3rd Quadrant:
Implementation
Getting along with people
Delivery focus

CEO

COO

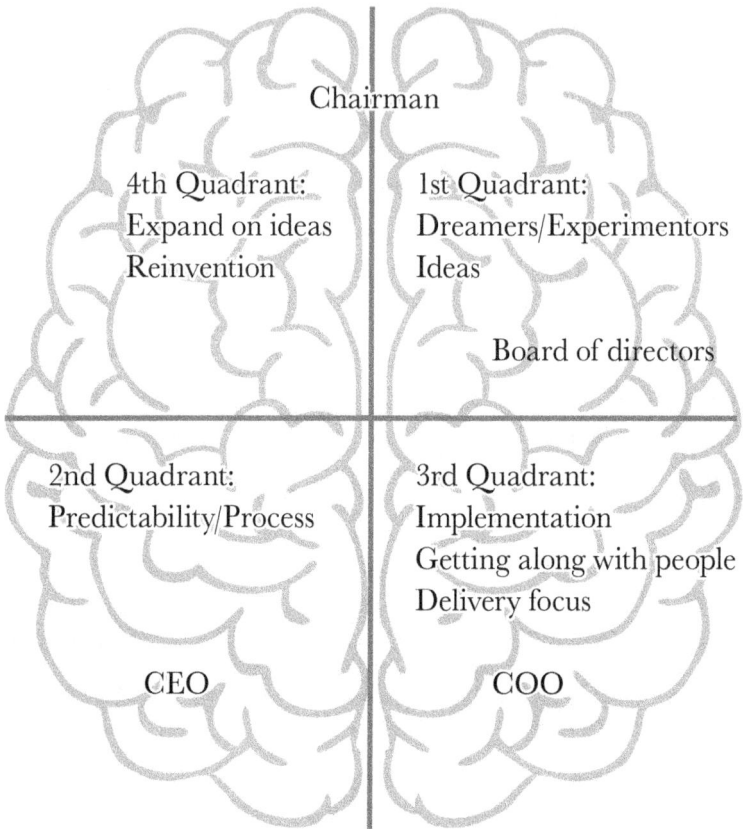

- At top left, you have the "so what" part of the brain, covering how you process information with intuition and gut feeling.
- At top right, you have the "board brain", which is all about creativity and seeing the big picture.
- At bottom left is the "CEO brain", which is all about analysis (How do I deal with the fluff that the top right quadrant just gave me?).

- And finally at the bottom right is your "COO brain", which is all about relationships and implementation (What do I do with the information that the bottom left just told me?).
- What does that mean in terms of people's wiring, and how could we put a set of executives or a company into that?

I've been privileged to speak with Dr Mark Postles (the creator of the in8model), who corroborated my experiences that we all have a conceptual preference in wiring and its meaning. We've both found that if you imagine the very top of the brain (which would be the chairman of the company), they'd be navigating between the intuitive and the creative. The board, on the other hand, is all about coming up with big ideas (How are we going to move to Mars next week? How are we going to create an aeroplane?) and focus on that. So, it's more of a big picture.

To go into slightly more detail, the bottom left is all about the analytical. This equates to a typical CEO, whose skills involve organisation. (How do we make the decision? How do we move the company forward to translate the big picture into actionable items?) It's the board that makes this idea implementable.

On the bottom right is the relational quadrant, which concerns getting along with people and making things move forward. You can also find human resources (HR) there. The top part of the brain is all about the board – the very senior function. The bottom left equates to the CEO, while the bottom right resembles the COO.

Now, what does that mean practically? If your boss sits very heavily in the top quadrant, you might imagine a COO (who's all about relationships) making things happen, creating change management, and implementing the change. Remember, these quadrants are just preferences – I'm not professing that we're going to put people in rigid boxes that they can't move out of.

So, it's not about saying: "I'm this. I'm not that". Instead, it's more about our preferences, because we all have these parts of the brain. If you're obsessed with a very big idea, you can start talking a very, very different language.

Let me give you an example. Picture a quarterly meeting between the CEO, COO and chief financial officer (CFO), where the agenda is to review how the business is running (nothing too controversial). The CFO opens with how the numbers aren't great, how costs are higher than revenues, how IT (for example) is spending too much money on the application, and so on.

The CEO is turning to the COO, angry that his strategy hasn't been delivered yet, and wondering why we haven't captured more market share and why the competition is doing much better than our company. When the COO gets a chance to respond, they might say that we need people to generate revenues as the targets are overly high. They may add that the IT platform is indeed coming along well, but the return on investment (ROI) will only happen post–roll out and the numbers need to get worse before they get better. (This could be a comedy if it wasn't a frequent occurrence in meetings.) Ironically, even though the 3 "C levels" (COO, CFO, CEO) are aiming at exactly the same target, they have such distinctive ways of expressing themselves that the others might as well be from a different planet.

What's even more interesting is that neither can see where the others are coming from. So, when asked to "go to Mars", a COO will respond: "No, it has to be feasible; it has to be implementable. And forget going to Mars; we need the aeroplane. Actually, forget the aeroplane; we need a blueprint. Let's do a prototype". If you're an impatient CEO or board, you'll be thinking something like: "Well why do I need to know that? I don't need a blueprint or a plan – just get it done". You can start seeing big differences in the way each sector thinks.

As an exercise, imagine swapping places with someone with a different role for five minutes. This will help you see things from another perspective.

If you're usually very details-focused, imagine not being able to pay any attention to detail from now on. I don't know if you've ever seen a book called *Where's Wally?*, where you have to find a character (Wally) on a double page of people crowded together. A CEO could probably number them and provide other details, but may not be able to find Wally! Sometimes, you need to completely change the way you think.

Now let's take it even further. How do you change the way you *talk*? For example, imagine a very detailed and logical person from an engineering background, for whom emotions, intuition, and a big-picture perspective play a very small role in their day-to-day thinking. How would they then communicate to their boss, who might think very differently? They would need to choose specific words for situations involving communication, so they could start talking a language both parties can understand.

In theory, this is easy to do, but in reality it's quite difficult. In my role as a leader, I've virtually had to do translation courses to help highly competent managers or individual contributors learn a new language so that they can communicate with the CEO or a board who doesn't really care about the nuts and bolts. In my example, how many nuts does it take to build the wing of an aeroplane? The board couldn't care less. What they'll care about is how fast it can go, what it looks like, and where it will travel to. So, while it's a mental struggle to find suitable words, being able to do this will help you grow within the company and navigate ways to move outside your preferred quadrant to start talking the language of other quadrants. When playing the corporate game, you need to teach people to navigate different quadrants rather than staying where they prefer to be. To be effective, they need to be where the audience is.

Let's break this up into smaller chunks.

The boardbrain can think about the big picture. (In Mark Postles' in8model, it's located in the top right corner.) Their job is to dream big, experiment, and come up with big ideas. Details and how to get things done don't come anywhere near the top of their agenda. They're the "Let's go to Mars tomorrow" people.

The CEO brain (bottom left in in8model) is all about organising, creating predictability and processes. They'll be all about "What do we need to do to create a rocket, then ensure it flies 100% of the time?".

The COO brain (bottom right in in8model) will worry about practical implementation, such as how to ensure people work together to deliver the project.

In smaller companies, I've observed that there's often an overlap between different needs. For example, the CEO and board have very similar skillsets, as do the COO and CEO.

In one company I worked for, the CEO decided we were going to implement AI immediately because it had such incredible potential. His rationale? We'll make fewer mistakes and be more technologically focused. However, our infrastructure couldn't cope with that.

In the Appendix, you'll find an exercise which challenges a details-focused person to describe a picture from a 50,000-foot level of detail, helping people understand it without getting too intricate. If you're a very big picture person, I challenge you to start understanding the picture in intricate detail. What does that information tell you? How can you use it to your advantage? And how can you see the big differences between the big picture and the details without overlooking the beauty of either the big picture or the detail?

For this to work, you have to remember to walk in the other person's shoes from time to time. You don't have to change your brain and how it works, but only remember how it's different. This will help you tailor your own way of talking and find a middle ground.

Watch out for the big shifts when you go from a COO to a CEO position, including the details. Are you going to be a big picture or a detail-oriented person? Another way to describe it is a bit like a sculpture or a garden. If you're going to sculpt a piece of marble, you'll create the rough edges of the sculpture before refining, and refining, and refining. (Consider the difference between ten bullet points (big-picture) and five pages (detail-oriented). If you decide to make the switch from one road to another, a shift of thinking will be necessary – and it can be done.

Is there a map? Yes!

CEO	COO
Loves the big picture, strategy, and the long term, but doesn't worry about how to get there.	Focuses on the "how", less worried about the big picture than how to implement it.
Worst nightmare is daily/weekly run of the business update to take the pulse of the company.	Can't live without understanding how implementation is progressing and keeping a "finger on the pulse" at all times.
Tends to be more focused on a few big objectives.	Day is spent juggling 1,000 balls, constantly focusing on day-to-day operations, its details, and the people making it happen.
Dislikes involvement, perfectionists, and being controlled.	Practical, steady, stabilises environment, works in the business.

Neither is wrong.

Remember, different wiring means a totally different way of thinking. It *doesn't* mean that one is right and the other is wrong. Both are valid. And it's all about knowing yourself and how to communicate with a person with the opposite wiring. Yes, they're different – but they can also work incredibly well together. Magic can happen, and I've been privileged during my career to work with CEOs worldwide who think completely differently than me, but we had an understanding of each other's wiring and used it to our strength. I can't imagine how to create a rocket to go to Mars, but I *can* make sure I build it damn well. And we use those strengths and different ways of thinking to accomplish great things.

So now that we understand that not everyone thinks the same way, and you've seen ways to make the most of that, what about being invisible or too nice? We'll look at that in the next chapter.

CHAPTER 4

ARE YOU TOO NICE, TOO QUIET, OR TOO ANYTHING?

OR, JUST PERFECT AS YOU ARE?

Have you ever been told you are too much of something? Too quiet, too loud, or too verbose, or just too something else? You don't add enough in the meetings, you don't talk enough, you don't participate enough. I can't hear you enough. You're not in my face enough.

I have. I've heard it happen to a lot of other people too. Do they have a point, or is some of this innate and unchangeable?

By the end of the chapter, you'll understand your core values and what you stand for. You'll have a baseline of what you're willing to change or take feedback on, and when you're not willing to (and shouldn't) change.

One day, I was listening to best-selling author and motivational speaker Simon Sinek. He introduced the concept of coins, which really resonated with me. It goes something like this.

An introvert starts the day with five coins. Every time they have a conversation, they spend one of their coins. On the other hand, an extrovert starts the day with zero coins. Every time an extrovert has a conversation, they *gain* a coin. What tends to happen – and I've seen this both with myself and with many of my coaching clients – is that an introvert is exhausted by the end of the day,. The *last* thing they want to do is talk to people. That doesn't make you a lesser person, it just means you've spent all your coins. On the other hand, the extrovert will be buzzing by the end of the day. They'll want to talk to you and have a conversation. And if you're an introvert with a spouse who's an extrovert, they'll want to tell you all about their day in intricate detail, while all you want is some quiet time to recover.

Confusing introversion with shyness is dangerous, as they're very different. For example, a very good friend and colleague of mine is very introverted like me. Neither of us love public speaking, yet we can do it when we really need to. We're not afraid to organise an impromptu meeting with a large team, speak to them, and get grilled with a barrage of questions when the topic is difficult. Fear isn't part of this equation. It's more about "enjoyment of the meeting" and its impact on our energy levels.

Shyness, on the other hand, is more of a fear of being judged. It's rarely positive, and can lead to anxiety.

Let me explain how being shy can manifest. I was coaching a client who told me, "I really don't like talking in meetings or even bigger crowds because I'm shy". Whilst I understood the meaning of shy, I asked him: "What does being shy mean to you?". It transpired was that being shy, for him, was a cover for imposter syndrome. That incredibly successful client was worried that he wasn't good enough to talk, and that people would think badly about him; in fact, it was actually the other way around. After several sessions, we turned his "shyness" to butterflies of excitement before speaking; he moved from hating public speaking to enjoying it, though he was still nervous right before the start. In a life-changing moment for him, after overcoming his fear and sharing his passion and knowledge, his audience told him how much they relate to his story and how valuable it had been for them.

So, how does this work in a company? One of the teams I was running in the past was a major sales team. In most sales teams, people tend to be extroverts by definition. As I've mentioned, I'm more of an introvert. However, when we need to tighten up the sales team and meet our targets, I need to motivate them for the day (and even the week) to come. To do this, my friend and I had to get onto the floor, get out of our comfort zones, and temporarily become extroverts – well, not become extroverts *per se*, but get out of our comfort zone by pushing our sales guy to shine. Using the coin example, that meeting cost us some of our coins and depleted our energy reserves. Practically (and I know it's not always possible to choose the time), holding some of those meetings at the end of a working day would be much more difficult for me than holding them in the morning.

Let's dive deeper – where it all comes down to values.

We're now going to take this a little bit further and discover what you *can* change and what you *can't* or *won't* change. There's a huge difference between them. Many times, I've been told that I'm too quiet in meetings. Ironically, the feedback was coming from mega-extroverts; as we'll see in a following chapter, they didn't command the room but rather *took over* the room. When you're looking at the things you can and can't change, it's important to understand what your internal territory is, what's important to you, and who you are. My internal territory is a place where all my rules and values stem from. It's a place only visible to those really close to me, where external distractions are absent.

What makes you … you? You might think it is as simple as "I'm a good person" or "I like dancing and cooking", but unfortunately it's a bit more complex than this. I don't have a PhD in psychology, so let's keep it simple by categorising this into three buckets:

- **Traits** are like the foundation of the house. Without their strength, there is no house.
- **Values** are like the walls. Depending on which country you're in, they might be made of different materials to suit the environment.

- **Behaviour** is how you *respond* to the environment. In our house example, imagine you planted a tree in the garden. Today is very windy. How will your tree react? Will it bend or stay sturdy, no matter how strong the wind is?

I know it might sound like a lot to take in, but we're going to go slowly. If you want more details, we've created a questionnaire you'll find in Appendix 2. (By using myself as an example, I'll show you how it works.)

Traits, values and behaviours are three different concepts related to human psychology and personality, each with their own characteristics and functions.

Traits are relatively stable, referring to the enduring characteristics or qualities defining an individual personality. Consistent patterns of thinking, feeling, or behaviour distinguish one person from another, such as introversion, extroversion, conscientiousness, agreeableness, and openness to experiences. These traits describe how a person typically interacts with the world and others.

Your turn now … What are your top three traits or building blocks? What defines you at your core so that, no matter what, you're not willing to compromise? List them, then explain why they're so important to you. (**Remember:** They're like the **foundations** of your house, so strong nothing will ever change them.)

Values are important beliefs in principles and ideas. They represent what a person considers to be morally, ethically, or personally significant in life, guiding their decision-making and behaviour. Values can vary widely between individuals and cultures, and can include honesty, integrity, family, freedom, and social justice.

Your turn now … What are your top three values? What is important to you? List them, then explain why they matter to you. (**Remember:** they're like the **walls** of your house.) If you do this exercise with a friend, you might have the same foundations but very different walls, depending on where your house is built.

Behaviour refers to an observable action, such as an individual's response or conduct in a particular situation. That includes both conscious and subconscious reactions to external stimulants. Whilst strengths and value may provide a framework to understand behaviour, behaviour is the outward expression of an individual's thoughts, feelings, and intentions relating to specific situations.

Your turn now … What are your top three behaviours? What is your preferred way to react when something happens (interruptions, changes …?). Write them down to help you know yourself. (**Remember:** they're like the **trees** of your garden.) If you do this with a friend, you both might have incredibly different answers yet still be right.

Let me use myself as an example of what this can mean in terms of traits, values and behaviours. My **trait**, which I could unsuccessfully try to change for the rest of my life, is introversion. If we refer to Simon Sinek's coin analogy, I have my set number of coins, many of which will be used during the day. This means that evening networking, for example, isn't my favourite thing. When I have to network, I need to really dig deep into my coin bag.

If I were to describe myself in terms of **values**, I'd choose integrity. For me, it's black and white. If you ask me to break my integrity, this goes completely against my values; I'd rather refuse to do it, or escape the situation that's asking me to violate this value.

And finally, **behaviour.** My example is standing my ground if something is forcing me to compromise my integrity.

Let's see how this can shape meetings or life events.

Many years ago, I was honoured to be asked to judge a pres-tigious international event about business improvements, including who generated the biggest change in the bottom line. My boss had a friend at another company who'd entered this contest, and asked me directly to "help" their friend win. This went completely against my value of integrity. And whilst I'm not advocating that *everyone* should do what I did, it went so far against my values that I resigned instead of changing the score to make my boss's friend win. This is an example of how my own values dictate my decisions, and how I'll approach a situation based on what matters to me.

I hope this example helps you understand what we mean by traits, values, and behaviours. We've also learned that while traits are immovable, behaviour can change based on the situation; after all, the human brain is highly adaptable.

During my coaching sessions, some of my clients experience a set of emotions ranging from unease to extreme discomfort; in some cases, they even experience physical reactions (like stress) with their work. I often used a similar approach to help them understand what's causing it. In most cases, their work conflicts with their values or behaviours. When that happens, we work together to see how we can create alignment between them. (For example, do they need to be more patient with their boss, or more curious when a language barrier leads them to the wrong decision?)

However, I've also encountered clients where the clash goes much deeper, conflicting with their own core. Most of the time, this is harder to identify and takes longer to work on. I've never helped a client change their core, as I don't believe this is possible. When this happens, my work as a coach has been to help my client identify what needs to go, and how to make this happen. This can take many shapes, such as helping them with a career change or giving them interview practice. If the clash between the company and my client was at the level of traits, and the boss's behaviour was abusive, it may leave scars which will require healing before my client can move forward.

You might be wondering where I'm going with this, and why I included the journey of self-discovery. I request that you ask one of your friends or direct reports to take the same exercise and compare answers. As a leader, your job is to help get the best out of your teams, even where their values are different to yours. Imagine your value is "Be the best at work so your career can reach stellar levels", while that of your direct report is "Family comes first". How do you deal with this? Both of you have potentially opposite values, or those which have differing effects on the workplace. The way I dealt with this was to ensure the work and its schedule matched the priorities of my employee. When we achieved that equilibrium, I had a happy, dedicated employee who gave me their best. Whilst it's not always possible to change the work schedule, what *is* possible as a leader is to decide how much you're willing to do and how creative you want to be. While one of my family-oriented employees had no choice but to be "on-call" at night, receiving a "work from home day" or an extra day off meant a lot more than additional money as compensation for unsociable work hours. Value-based rewards go much further than money. You're clearly showing you understand your team and what matters to them.

Hopefully, by now you have a much better understanding of your foundations, including what they mean to you and how you'll react in specific situations. Remember, there are no perfect answers, and the beauty is that they're all different.

Leadership is about getting the best out of those differences and using them as strengths to create a high-performing team, not as a dividing mechanism. If you were to give the questionnaire you've taken to the whole of your teams and direct/indirect reports, it's highly likely everyone would have different answers. That's the beauty of it. As a leader, one of your main strengths will be how you use people's different qualities to achieve the task and the KPIs being assigned.

Have you been in a situation where change was needed for you to progress to the next level, manage a bigger team, or get that promotion you so want? Our next chapter will help you build your brand to become more in tune with your dreams.

CHAPTER 5

YOU ARE NOT VISIBLE ENOUGH

EVER HEARD OF SASHA FIERCE? YOU MIGHT KNOW HER AS BEYONCÉ.

Recently, whilst I was watching a movie, a quote from Batman/Bruce Wayne really inspired me: "It is not who I am underneath, but what I do, that defines me".

In this chapter, you'll learn how to create a personal brand, what it takes to make it stick, and the benefit of having multiple brands (and knowing when to use them). One of the things I often hear from my coaching clients is: "I let my work do the talking. And why should I have a personal brand? I'm not a company. What people see is what people get". If those sound familiar, then you're reading the right chapter.

What makes personal branding relevant to everyone is that we have two "business cards" in a way: the one we know about and the one we don't. The first business card is the one we control (or believe we do), which we use to consciously project traits or characteristics onto other people. (For example, I work 24 hours a day because I want people to see I'm driven.) The second is much more subtle. It's the one we might not be conscious of projecting, but people see nevertheless. (For example, if you work all the time and expect everyone else to do the same, people around you might see you as someone with no work–life balance who doesn't care about those with families.)

Many people I interact with have been incredibly competent when they only had themselves to manage, but became underperformers nearly overnight when given a team to manage. They moved from loving their job to absolutely hating it, feeling totally inadequate as they weren't prepared to deal with the new situation in which they found themselves. This is a clash of personal branding traits or behaviours. This happens because you have to move from a small ecosystem of you and your manager to a totally new one, where each step is now the result of many influences. (This is why a 360-degree review is a great tool to assess your own brand.) If you're a bad leader, your team will complain to HR; if you're a bad team player, your peers will instantly put roadblocks in your way and potentially escalate matters to your boss. Based on my experience, companies or leaders should have a "before you get promoted" training session, showcasing changes in the ecosystem. If someone refuses to be promoted as a result of that training, it's a good thing both for the company and the individual – for the company, because they won't have "forced managers" who lack other options; and for the individual, whose stress level will reduce.

Let me give you an example that resonates with many of my coaching clients. Many people know Starbucks, yet when prompted with the name 'Starbucks', very few people mentioned coffee. However, what everyone mentioned was the environment, the sofa, and how comfortable Starbucks are to work in. But they also know that anywhere they go in the world, they'll find that same feeling of comfort, that consistency. What does that tell you? Isn't it interesting that the biggest coffee brand in the world is known by so many people for something other than coffee? Doesn't that suggest a significant difference between the brand Starbucks portrays, and the brand others perceive?

Let's start by breaking down the branding into clear components. First, identify the unconscious brand you're projecting, and compare it to the brand you *believe* you have. As Amazon founder Jeff Bezos said, "Your personal brand is what people say about you after you leave the room". I like to do a brand audit exercise which goes like this: Ask three, four, or five people you know what are the first three words that spring to mind when **they** think about you – anyone will do (although preferably colleagues if you want to do your personal branding at work, or family and friends if you want to do it in non-work situations). Jot down their answers. Now, write down the first three words that spring to mind when **you** think about yourself and how you imagine people see you at work.

Compare these responses. How close are they to each other? What does it tell you? Are you perceived as loud, when you thought you were quiet? Or someone pushy, when you thought you were encouraging?

How do those really compare to your brand, or more importantly, the brand you *thought* you were projecting? In my eyes, your branding has a **conscious** and an **unconscious** component. Your conscious branding can include your dress sense (e.g. Are you fashion-conscious or traditional?), whilst the unconscious one is much more about what affect you and your brand that's really a blind spot when you think about yourself? In the exercise you've just completed, you wrote down your **conscious** brand (the one you're aware of). What your co-workers wrote down is your **unconscious** brand (what people see and feel about you). If they match, that's amazing. If not, what does your **unconscious** brand say about you – and do you want or need to address it?

One of my clients realised he wasn't focusing on meeting with clients enough. When we spoke about it during one of our sessions, it transpired that it was due to fear of not being good enough or not knowing what to speak about and being "found out". His vulnerabilities were really holding him back. Unconsciously, his brand expressed: "I'm not driven, and would rather be behind my desk instead of in the field".

Now that you have your unconscious brand, let's move to the more conscious level and identify the attributes you need to create your new brand. This should be based on your specific situation, but also on your values. What are you willing – and unwilling – to change?

For example, one of my coaching clients (let's call him Paul) really wanted a promotion to director level. Paul's a nice person who cares passionately about his team, but he can't say no. He'd accept work from management, but wouldn't delegate it to his team. Being so overloaded by work didn't allow him to focus on more strategic issues, as he should've done.

I've been told many times that I'm not loud enough in meetings, and asked why I don't talk more. The answer is simple. Because I'm an introvert, I prefer to ask others in the meeting to talk first, so I can understand where they're coming from. This allows me to process the information they've shared, then formulate my opinion.

I'm sharing this with you to reveal whether I'm willing to change the brand I share with people based on feedback. In my case, I'm not. It made no sense to me to become the loudest person in the room, because the loudest isn't necessarily right.

One of the many people I worked with *was* the "loudest person in the room". Interestingly, he never realised this, as he was expected to be loud in his previous job. It was very simple for him to understand that one size doesn't fit all – he can still be driven, targeted, and high-achieving without having to be the loudest.

If you start thinking about yourself and who you are at work, what does it take to get you to the next level? What kind of values does your job require to make sure you're successful in that promotion? When considering a new job with a different company, how do they compare with your values?

Remember, a **value** is something we don't really want to change. So, knowing what's required from you for the next level, where do you sit regarding that willingness to change?

Let's gently approach the next step now. You've found your brand and your values, and identified what you're willing to change. But how do you make it stick?

The best way to make your brand stick is consistency and repetition. It's a bit like learning to ride a bike. Not many people wake up one beautiful morning knowing how to ride the bike in their sleep. What can you practise daily to make sure you embody the new brand? In my example, Paul needed to start saying no and delegate to his team. One of the ways we helped him practise was by creating an accountability partner for Paul. When Paul started to say, "Yes, of course," the accountability partner would just nudge him and say, "Paul, remember, 'no' doesn't mean you're being unkind to the person. 'No' means you have boundaries, and only have 24 hours in a day". And it's hard – a bit like learning a new language. But consistency and repetition, with an accountability partner, coach, or mentor, will help you embed the change you want to implement.

Another trick I've given to some of my coaching clients is to ask: What if it's not you anymore, but you simply need a change? By asking "What if it's not you anymore?", I'm not suggesting to go completely against the values that define you. However, there's another tool you can use – creating an alter ego, then flipping between the different personalities.

Just like in the chapter about Sasha Fierce and Beyoncé, you can also create an alter ego. And during many coaching sessions, we've created alter egos with clients to help them – for example, in meetings. Imagine you're in a meeting, partnered to a successful consultancy company. You have to talk, because all eyes are on you. (This isn't because people want to make you anxious, but because they value your technical expertise.)

Your alter ego is the new person you can switch to when you have to do something that's not your preference, such as talking at meetings. Having an alter ego doesn't mean "cheating" on your own values or becoming someone you aren't. Research has demonstrated that some of the benefits of alter egos include helping individuals overcome limiting beliefs and negative self-talk. By embodying a powerful alter ego, individuals can shift their mindset and beliefs about themselves, leading to improved performance. I, for one, have an alter ego when I coach. I'm consciously calm, focused on listening without judging or asking myself: "What will I answer next?". What I *don't* have, as it would make no sense, is an alter ego who's my exact opposite. (For example, becoming super-extroverted wouldn't sit well, and there's no reason I'd want to do this.)

I had a client who struggled to move from work mode to home mode, daddy mode, and husband mode when he got home after a long day at work. We used something his children had created for him – a small bracelet. I asked him to leave it near the front door, then put it on when he arrived home. The physical act of putting the bracelet on created an alter ego: "I'm now a dad, and I need to play with my small children, be nice to my wife, leave the work behind".

Now let's explore another scenario: What happens if the change is demanded or requested, but it doesn't sit well with you? Let's come back to an earlier example: Imagine you're an extroverted team leader. You're loud in every sense of the term (and remember, there's nothing wrong with that), but your extroversion is dwarfing your team. Without you realising it, they find you so overpowering that they can't speak to you. Imagine we have a one-to-one, and this is the feedback I just gave you. Shocked, you're processing it and wondering what to do with it. Again, there's multiple ways to proceed. One of my favourites is creating a pros and cons list, which will help you by writing down the positives and negatives of the change. If you can't win, you have to decide what's more important to you. Is it the situation, or is it your values? In the example I used earlier of my boss asking me to change the result of scoring for their friend, it was clear to me that what mattered more for me was my own integrity. And this is why, as I mentioned earlier, I chose to resign from the job. Again, I'm not emphasising that *everyone* needs to resign. In my example, I did a pros and cons list – this doesn't have to be pages and pages long, as it's about the strength of each point. Any point that would compromise my integrity is a deal-breaker, leaving only two options: Either the cause of the situation needs to be resolved, or I need to extract myself from it.

Hopefully this chapter has helped you understand a bit more about personal branding, and the fact that *everyone* has a personal brand, whether we like it or not. Think about it: How often do you enter the room and make a snap judgement about the people in it, even if you've never met them? So, the key to creating a new brand lies in the fact that it can be compared to a marathon, not a sprint. Repetition and conscious embodying of the brand takes time and effort. Be prepared for setbacks and bumps in the road. But remember that no brand was created in one day, and no-one can say, "We've had no problem when creating our brand".

Again, to come back to the example above, many people I coach, and have helped in the past, have told me, "I don't need a brand", or "I don't have a brand". Nothing can be further from the truth. We all do. People always have, and always will, pass judgement. What if we consciously took steps to ensure we leave the right impression, instead of leaving it to chance? The life of your personal brands (or one of your brands) will greatly vary, based on what you use it for. The grandad, husband, or partner brand will last much longer than the "I just need to pass that interview" brand. Keep practising to make sure you truly embody the you that you *want* people to see. One of the main instances when brand management becomes crucial is during meetings. Are you taking over the room, or commanding it? Are people avidly listening to you, or falling asleep after your one-minute answer?

CHAPTER 6

CAN YOU COMMAND THE ROOM?

WITHOUT TAKING IT OVER?

I've spent a lot of time thinking about how I want to present myself as a leader and an executive. I think it's a valuable thing for all of us to think about, though it may not be top of mind for most.

Have you ever been in a meeting when someone's so outspoken and overbearing that no-one else gets a say? They take the meeting over, and everyone's thinking, "What on earth was that?". I'd suggest it's not a good thing. This isn't a stage for you to steal the limelight and shut down ideas and other voices.

Yet there's a way you can command the room without taking it over. I believe it's one of the most useful skills a leader can master. Why? In the previous chapter, we spoke about conscious and unconscious brands. When you're on the receiving end, there's a fundamental difference between someone who's driven and someone who's overbearing. The irony is that most of the people who are overbearing don't realise it. For the small majority who do it consciously, this is a totally different discussion about leadership style.

In this chapter, you'll learn the difference between commanding the room and dominating it. You'll learn how to project confidence, command the room without shouting, and allow people to speak without dwarfing them. You'll enable them to come out of their shell and share their ideas to help you fix the problem. And you'll learn how to command the room, even if you're painfully quiet.

Twenty years ago, I was working for a huge bank when the production system went down. We were losing thousands of pounds per minute. We called an emergency meeting where every single division was present, and it was total chaos. People were shouting, pointing fingers, "It's not me, it's because *they* did" … the usual. At some point, someone had the brilliant idea to call one of the senior people. That was the benefit of anonymity: "We'll call John".

When John arrived, the first thing people said was, "John is in the room". Even the people on the phone felt John's presence. When John entered, the room went quiet. That's when I learned how to command the room. What was so different about him? What made him who he was? How did he manage to enter the room and have the presence to bring things down without saying a single word? That was the magic of John. So, what's the recipe? How did he do it?

Step 1: What's the first thing you're projecting when you enter the room? Is it confidence? Is it stress? What you project doesn't have to be who you are. I'm sure John was stressed. So, how do you manage to be in control of your emotions, or at least hide them enough so that people don't see what you're truly feeling? One of the things I keep remembering is that – at least in the work I do – no-one's going to die. Also, as a data-driven person, when I enter the room in one of those situations, I know very little, and I need the people in the room to help me. This means that I'm not the most valuable person in the room. *Everyone* is. I hope this makes people feel important, like John made all of us feel that day.

Step 2: How are you going to approach a topic? What are your first couple of sentences going to be, and what are they going to achieve? Are you going to blame people, or reassure them? Are you going to look for information? One of the first things John said when he entered that room was, "Hi everyone, how's everyone doing?". This sounds very simple and petty (especially as the bank was losing money) – but if you think about it, the first thing he did was make it personal. How can you as a leader break the ice and remind people, "We're in this together"?

Step 3: Consider your tone. Commanding the room doesn't mean shouting the loudest. Allow me to share two relevant stories. The first involves my psychology teacher while I was completing my degree. If you can imagine an empty theatre with 300 or 400 students, it can be pretty loud in the break between the courses. Yet he'd never raise his voice and decided he didn't need a microphone. Instead, he'd enter and wait a minute or two for the class to settle down. And if they didn't, he'd just speak like you and I speak. Magically, without raising his voice, the noise would go down quickly because people wanted to hear what he had to say.

I've also been in rooms when things are tense, and the opposite of a John comes in and starts screaming. These first minutes can be crucial in influencing how the rest of the meeting goes and what emotions people will feel. Shouting, I'm sure, made the person feel better, or at least less frustrated, but it also completely destroyed the mood in the room. Instead of people opening up and admitting what they did was wrong or a mistake of the department – and with that admission, helping people to fix the problem – they instantly became very guarded. No-one wanted to share anything; it was each to their own. "Let's just be quiet, so hopefully we don't get shouted at" was the main sentiment.

The second ingredient of what made John so incredible is that he wasn't interested in what caused the issue or the minute tasks that would need to be done to fix it. What he *was* interested in was leading people by having them follow him. And what better way to do this than becoming a coach, or becoming the person who just started a new job and wants to learn more about it? Commanding the room didn't mean shouting the loudest … instead, all John did was ask the right question. This wasn't "Who's done this?"; instead, it was "What's the problem?". Choosing the right question can either make people feel the shame of blame, or make them feel part of the solution. In a way, the question *is* the answer.

So, how can you take control as a leader if you only ask questions? Because, if you think about it, as a leader, it's highly unlikely you'll have the technical knowledge represented by all the departments who are in the room trying to fix the problem. If you experience a problem in IT or banking, for example, there will be many topics you probably don't know about.

In this situation, the question can no longer be "Who?", but is instead "What?". In my experience, "Why" questions, such as "Why did you do that?", are also unhelpful. If the person knew what was going to happen, it's pretty likely they wouldn't have done it. So, questions like, "What's the problem?" and "How do we move it forward?" are more effective. In asking those questions as a leader, your role becomes much more of a facilitator or a coach than of a manager. *Psychology Today* defines coaching as "a process that aims to help clients achieve concrete goals, identify and overcome obstacles to wellbeing and performance, and build skills that may be interfering with their success ... psychological coaching concentrates on individual or group strengths and abilities and how they might be used in new and different ways to enhance performance, feel better about the self, ensure smooth life transitions, strengthen relationships, deal with challenges, achieve goals, become more successful". This is, in my opinion, what made John truly outstanding and allowed him to have true command of the room. Most of the senior people

I've known who truly are leaders display similar traits. They were coaching the room, and the room followed instead of them having to take over the meeting.

In a way, the worst thing you can be is a micromanager, saying things like, "Okay, John, yep, thanks, done. Alan, okay, great. When are you going to do that?" ... At this point, the room is looking up to you for calm. It's a bit like the ship looking up to the Captain and gauging what he's thinking. Your role is stewardship and leadership, which will help people relax and move on from the panic. If you think about the brain's "fight or flight" centre – the amygdala – people are probably experiencing one of these emotions at this point. Let me quickly elaborate. Our amygdala has been programmed over thousands of years to react in a few ways when in the presence of a perceived danger: either fight the danger (in this case, no-one will want to pick a fight with someone senior screaming in the room) or flee from it (i.e. run away), which is highly likely to be what goes through people's minds at this point. By staying calm and in control, you're projecting calm, so the brain realises this is not a "dangerous" situation and can be tackled. Projecting calmness helps people regain control, which will enable them to use their specialist knowledge to solve the problem.

Finally, when you've gone around the table enough times to understand what the problem is, what can be done about it, how you're going to implement the solution, and what the road ahead will be, your job as a leader when you're in command is only: "What can I do to help?".

This simple question makes people realise they have someone on their side. Being on their side and being the roadblock remover is the best thing leaders can do in those situations. As a leader, you have the magic wand to help your team make things happen. That's why you're the leader, and they report to you. So, the question then becomes: How will you use this quality to help the team realise you're on their side, not against them?

John impacted me for many years and, to this day, after nearly thirty years, I still aspire to be like him. Many people have told me I'm similar to John, but the way he impacted me made me realise that with leadership comes a huge responsibility in the sense that people look up to you instantly to see what mood you're in and take their cues from you.

In my opinion, John wasn't only an amazing leader; he also understood the value of emotional intelligence. This is one of the **keys to successful leadership:** The ability to be in control of your emotions will make or break you as a leader. You're no longer only responsible for yourself, but also for your team. If you panic, *they* panic; if you're calm, *they* stay calm. Emotional intelligence doesn't mean being emotionless and robotic; it means being able to recognise and control the impact of emotions on other people. It's helped me understand the powerful value of calm in the storm, and that how I speak and what I say can be a game-changer in any situation. One of the things my team has told me since then is that they've never seen me shout. This is not because I'm a better person and I never shout, but because I have a mental recipe that when I enter the room, I'm mentally prepared for the worst and can only be pleasantly surprised.

I've also been in meetings with "anti-Johns", where the leader's modus operandi is to scream at people and blame them. I've also seen leaders calling their staff extremely derogatory names in public. This has served me well in a way, as I soon learned how *not* to behave. If you call one of your direct reports a derogatory name or shout at them in public, you've instantly lost their loyalty. The first thing they'll do is start looking for another job. In the short term, the first thing they'll do is close up like an oyster, no longer wanting to share information – because then they know if they share information with you, they're going to get shouted at. *Knowledge at Wharton*, a business journal from the University of Pennsylvania's Wharton School, published an interesting article[1] about employee loyalty. It highlights that loyalty first has to be seen as reciprocal in the employee–employer relationship; it's give and take. What was even more interesting was that whilst employees are loyal to companies, they're mainly loyal to individuals. The article quotes management professor Matthew Bidwell's observation that "Employees are often more loyal to those around them — their manager, their colleagues, maybe their clients. These employees have a sense of professionalism — and loyalty — that relates to the work they do more than to the company".

---

1   https://knowledge.wharton.upenn.edu/article/declining-employee
     -loyalty-a-casualty-of-the-new-workplace/

So it comes down to, "Who do you want to be?". Do you want to be the John or the anti-John? And if you think about it, you really have to be in control of the only thing you can be in control of, and that's you. And it's also about, "How do we make sure that the environment or the event takes over?". It's all about self-control, and what techniques you use to keep it. Remember, the first thing people are going to do is look at you. If you scream, they'll think it's okay to scream, and they'll then scream at their team; if you blame, they'll think it's okay to blame and will then be quick to blame others. The things you say can make or break the whole company.

As you'll remember, your brand is what people say when you leave the room. Do you want people to think the moment that you've left the room, "Wow, that was intense!" or "Wow, I'm glad they've gone"?

Ensuring that a change you're implementing sticks isn't easy. It requires repetition (especially when one doesn't really want to) and reinforcement to make it a habit. One of many reasons why my clients gain a lot from coaching is that they have someone there to hold them accountable to what they've committed to. Whilst coaching is an incredibly powerful tool, it's not always possible to have your coach next to you 24/7. Another helpful technique is choosing an "accountability buddy". Whilst there's no magic recipe to determine the perfect buddy, they need to have some common characteristics: there has to be deep-rooted trust between you, as your buddy will have to point out truths that at times might not be easy to hear. In addition, your buddy must help you break the habit you're trying to change, not fuel it. In our example, you don't want someone encouraging you to blast the people who are responsible for the problems "because they deserve it". Accountability buddies can help those in control, especially if you know you have a particular tendency. If you're extremely verbose, you can have someone next to you nudging you and saying, "Let's keep it short". And remember, there's a huge difference between commanding the room and taking it over. So you can choose – do you want to be John, or do you want to be the anti-John? Do you want to command the room, or do you want to take it over?

Situations can be extremely unpredictable. How can you be prepared for a crisis? Make a mental checklist of what being prepared looks like, so you can be John instead of anti-John. It might be that you take a deep breath, then ask for more information. There are many things that you can do to be prepared for the unexpected. In the next chapter, we'll learn about a pivotal skill in leadership and management – the art of having a difficult conversation.

CHAPTER 7

HAVING THE TOUGH CONVERSATION

*WITHOUT DESTROYING THE
PERSON'S CONFIDENCE.*

L et me start with a quote from Maya Angelou that resonated with me: "People will forget what you said, people
will forget what you did, but people will never forget how you
made them feel".

Simon Sinek once talked about a tough conversation about
negotiating a pay rise, and it made me think how different it
is for those who manage people. For me, the tough conversation is almost always, "I have to fire you, terminate your
employment, give you really bad news". Tough conversations
are part of business and can be daunting, both for the one
delivering it and for the one receiving it.

I've had to have a lot of these conversations over the years. If
you're an executive, you will too.

In this chapter, we'll discuss how to deliver bad news without
making it personal and harming the other person's self-belief.

Done poorly, these conversations have the potential to cause lifelong scars and damage someone's confidence. After thirty years of business, having dealt with people from many countries and walks of life, nationalities and cultures, I still remember the first time I had to terminate someone's employment. I was absolutely terrified. All the evidence showed it was the right thing to do for the business, but I had no idea how to do it.

No-one ever forgets the first time they've had to fire someone. There are, of course, some things I wish I knew first. After all, has anyone ever taken a course on how to fire someone? Helen is an amazing HR manager, the first HR manager I had the pleasure of working with. She gave me a tip that stuck with me for life: "Whilst this is an incredibly personal thing to do, *do not* make it about the person. (She emphasised the **do not**.) Remember that no matter how bad they're performing, they're human beings like you and me". This simple tip stayed with me forever, and I was thanked many times later, even by people whose employment I ended, that I did it humanely.

Do *not* make it about the person.

Corporate life has the potential to create many difficult conversations. From telling a stakeholder the project will be late to realising that we've gone over budget, there are many topics making for an unpleasant conversation. Terminating someone's employment isn't taught at school, and whilst I'm going to use employment termination as an example in this chapter, not all conversations are as tough as that. Judging by my own experience, and by that of the leaders who work for me, it's one of the hardest things managers do.

Delivering bad news is not something anyone likes doing, but I found that using four simple steps makes it a little easier.

Step 1: Prepare yourself for the conversation.

It's going to be a taxing time for you – mentally and emotionally. I use items like visualisation (this is when you imagine and visualise the situation as you want it to happen, including what might happen. You mentally go through it, creating a set of images or scenarios of how you want the discussion to happen) and scripting (which is when you have it scripted, a bit like dialog in a movie) to ensure I'm fully present in the moment.

Think about it. There are no *Being a Leader 101* or *How to Terminate Someone Nicely* books. So, for many people, it's all about learning by doing and hoping they did their best. As there's no magic wand, what technique can you use to prepare yourself for what's about to happen? One of the things that I remember from that very first instance is how drained I was by the end, even though it was the right thing to do. What's ironic is by the end of the HR meeting, the employee terminated said to me, "I knew it was coming. I'm okay with it". But I was still emotionally drained.

Whilst it somehow gets easier over time, it's never easy. Even at the end of my career, I still get butterflies when I have to terminate someone's employment. I still have to think: Is it the right thing? Am I 100% sure I've done my homework to make sure the person isn't going through a hard time personally?

I remember one of the times where someone was underperforming, and whilst we weren't going to go straight to termination, there was something wrong. So we had to have a performance conversation. It was only through that conversation that the person finally explained that they were going through an extremely difficult time. Because I was emotionally prepared, I started the conversation by asking a question about *them*. That completely changed the tone of the conversation and how it went.

Step 2: Be factual, not personal.

No matter how poorly the person is performing, it doesn't make them *bad*. Instead, it makes them unsuited for the job you ask them to do. A company can replace any of the workers, but the friends or family of that person cannot replace the person. What you say and how you make them feel could impact them for years.

Also, if you're terminating someone because of cost-cutting, let them know. It's very different to tell someone "We're terminating you because you're bad at your job", compared to

"We're terminating you because the company has to remove employees, otherwise it won't survive".

The way you approach a conversation has massive implications. Are you going to be a shouter, or are you going to speak quietly? I've witnessed both sides. Unfortunately, some of the clients I coach have dealt with managers who are shouters – or, if you remember the previous chapter, anti-Johns. An anti-John can destroy a person's confidence by focusing on the human being instead of the situation.

I vividly remember one of my coaching clients, who was the top performer in his company and doing extraordinarily well, still bearing the scars of bad conversations from ten years earlier. Consequently, that person has had to carry the scars of being shouted at with them for every day of their life. As I said, if someone is underperforming, it doesn't make them a bad person; it just means they're not suited for the job.

Step 3: Be ready for it.

By 'be ready for it', I don't mean have notes ready. For me, preparation is being prepared for a very large range of emotions, ranging from tears to anger. Many times, a person becomes emotional during the conversation. And whilst you're there to represent the company, it doesn't mean you can't be human. It doesn't mean you can start giving them a hug, but at the same time, it's OK to give them time to compose themselves. If they're angry, it's the same. Saying something like, "I can understand your anger" or "I sympathise with what you might be going through" has the potential to go a long way. But the key is, give them time. It's not easy to prepare for these conversations – I go over the upcoming meeting many times in my head, playing out all the possible scenarios from different angles. If it's potentially going to be extra-difficult, I'll even play it aloud, making mental notes to stay calm. By playing the conversation over and over in my head, it makes it less novel when it actually takes place. I know I'm ready for it, I'll be kind, and it won't affect my mental health. If the conversation really affects you, please remember you're not alone. You can always speak with your HR person, a coach, or a friend/colleague who understands you. In some of my coaching sessions, I've helped clients with those conversations by doing dry runs or role plays. As a coach, I've even played angry employees (or whatever helped my client most) to make the actual conversation less emotionally taxing.

This isn't a race for the fastest-ever conversation. It's something that, if you do it well, will allow them to have a positive experience in a bad situation. Also, remember it's a small world. There's a chance that in many years, the tables could turn. (You might become that person's employee, for example.)

So whenever you have those hard conversations, get ready for the full range of emotions. These can vary widely, depending on the individual's personal circumstances and coping mechanisms, but some common emotions include:

1. Shock and disbelief: Many people initially react with shock, and may have difficulty accepting the news of their job termination, especially if it comes as a surprise.
2. Anger and frustration: Feelings of anger and frustration are common reactions, often directed towards the employer, colleagues, or the circumstances that led to the termination.
3. Anxiety and fear: Losing a job can bring about financial insecurity and worries about the future, which can lead to anxiety and fear.
4. Sadness and grief: Losing a job can feel like a significant loss, and individuals may grieve the loss of their role, routine, and workplace connections.
5. Shame and embarrassment: Some individuals may feel a sense of shame or embarrassment about their job loss, even if it was due to factors beyond their control.
6. Relief: In some cases, people may experience a sense of relief if they were unhappy in their job or if the termination brings an end to a stressful or toxic work environment.
7. Uncertainty: The future may seem uncertain, and individuals may grapple with questions about their next steps, such as finding a new job, changing careers, or pursuing further education.
8. Self-doubt: Job loss can lead to feelings of self-doubt and a loss of self-esteem, particularly if the termination is perceived as a reflection of one's abilities.
9. Resilience and determination: Over time, many people find the strength to bounce back and use the experience as a motivator to search for new opportunities and make positive changes in their career.

It's important to note that these emotions are natural responses to job loss, and may not follow a linear progression. People may cycle through these emotions multiple times and at different intensities as they come to terms with the situation. Whilst you might not face all of them during the conversation, you might be faced with one or more, so you need to be mentally prepared to help the person deal with them.

Step 4: Do a final circle back ...
Have you missed something?

The next key item of the magic recipe, to call it that, starts with making the person talk and asking them questions like, "What's missing?" or "What are the challenges?", which might help you understand why they're not performing as they should. They might come with excuses, and if they do, this might help you either reconsider your decision or understand the reason why they can't do their job satisfactorily.

Let me give you two examples. In the first example, the person is performing extremely poorly and it's only in that conversation, which was very close to being the final conversation, that they let us know that a close family member was suffering from cancer. When asked why they didn't want to share it, we realised that they were a private person who didn't want to share it. But of course, it affected their performance.

The second example is the opposite. I remember being in a sales environment and having salespeople delivering terrible results. During the conversations when I asked, "What's going on? Why are you not performing? Is it a lack of training?", one person said to me, "Well, I've actually realised through the training and the management that selling isn't for me. It's not because I don't like the company. I've just realised I'm not a salesperson. I can't sell and I want to go back to a job where I don't sell".

If I'd been an anti-John shouting, the person would never have told me the main reason; they would've left the company with bad feelings as a result. This can have a detrimental effect on the company, as their words about their termination experience could harm the brand.

I can proudly say that all the people I've terminated have said that they'd love to work for me again in future. And it's not because I'm an extraordinary person – it's because of the preparation I did for those interviews and meetings.

Finally, if you're still convinced your decision is right after all of the above, explain your rationale in a direct unemotional way, such as: "The standards aren't met; the sales numbers aren't good enough"; and **not**: "You're lazy, you can't sell. What *are* you good at?". (I've seen both.)

As paradoxical as it sounds, even if you've terminated the person, offer to help them find a new job or give them a reference. As I said earlier, tomorrow they could be your boss in a new company, and you don't want to have burned your bridges.

Terminating someone can have a positive effect. Many years ago during a merger of two companies, I was in charge of terminating thousands of people. This became extremely taxing, but I still tried to do it well. Some of those people wanted to do something completely different, such as open a restaurant. Because we looked after them when they were terminated, they were able to follow their dreams and became incredibly successful.

If I'd terminated them on a bad note by implying they were bad people, the outcome would've been very different. In my coaching hub, I've seen countless people who have either been terminated or had poor performance appraisals. Around 90% of the time, this occurs for a couple of reasons.

The first one is about their personal performance. Why couldn't they do the job? If the tone is confrontational, or if the manager speaks much more than the employee, it nearly always becomes a lecture of how bad they are – very different from a performance appraisal.

As strange as it might sound, a performance appraisal meeting or termination can be an extremely constructive conversation if done well. And it can lead to the person flourishing in the next stage of their life.

Of course, your first difficult conversation will be the hardest. If you've never had a difficult conversation, I'd encourage you to practise it with a friend, your coach, or your HR manager. In my experience, this is the one meeting that you can't do unprepared. Never assume the second, third or fiftieth meeting is easier; instead, always prepare. Unfortunately, part of leading people – and this is definitely not taught at school – is having difficult or unpleasant conversations. As a leader, you decide the impact that the conversation will have.

Remember that the impact will not only be felt during those fifteen or thirty minutes, but could potentially be there for life. Keep an open mind. You might discover a key element about the person that could change your mind, and that's okay.

When reading the next chapter, imagine that one day, totally out of the blue, someone comes to you and says, "You're an inspiration to me". What would you do?

CHAPTER 8

WHAT DOES IT TAKE TO BE INSPIRATIONAL?

AND WHAT DOES IT DO TO THE PEOPLE AROUND YOU?

One of the quotes that resonates with me when I think about inspiration is from Peter Parker of *Spider-Man*: "With great power comes great responsibility". Being inspirational isn't a title you give yourself. Being inspirational is a reflection of consistency, selflessness, and servant leadership. (Servant leadership is a type of leadership where the leader is focusing on helping other people grow. It is all about "serving" others versus taking power or control of all situations.) Being inspirational also requires a great amount of self-confidence. For me personally, it becomes all about other people and no longer about me and looking for glory.

Many times during my career, I've been told, "You need to be more visible. It needs to be more about you". And I've always ignored it. I've always hated the limelight, being centre stage. Not because I have Imposter Syndrome, but because at heart, I genuinely feel my calling is to serve people, to help them be what they truly wish to be. That has always translated into boosting my team. At times, this comes at the cost of not boosting myself. For example, many times a very senior person has told me, "We know you like your team, we know you want to give them the credit, but it will also be good to for you to say, 'I did this', and we all know at senior level, that also means your team". That's never been me. For me, if my team does the work, they deserve the credit.

So imagine my shock when one day, during a one-on-one, someone told me I was inspirational, and explained how my management helped them grow further than they ever dreamed they could. In my view, though, all I did was my job. For me, it's much better to be interested than interesting. And by that, I also mean that I'd rather see someone else flourish than getting kudos myself. In my book, being truly inspirational isn't easy.

The first step is: Is it heartfelt? Are you confident enough in your abilities to park your ego at the door and start serving others? As an example, many years ago I started earning my rescue diver certificate. On that day, my instructor said something that was both mundane and deep: "Forget what you learn; that was to help yourself. Now learn to help others". For me, it really depends on your confidence; when you start helping people and putting others in front of you, you have to be confident in your own ability to know that you've been there, you've done that, and your worth is no longer questionable.

At this stage of my career, I feel I have nothing to prove to anyone anymore. And if anyone wants to question my abilities, my CV speaks for itself. So, first of all, be confident. And if you're not, that's okay – speak to someone who can objectively tell you, "Look at what you've done".

For many of my clients who reach a level where they want to be inspirational, I'm the person who can say, "Well, your LinkedIn profile speaks for itself", or "You've reached that level in your company. Surely this is not by luck". So, this is all about self-confidence and your ability to go, "Okay, it's no longer about me; it's all about someone else".

The second step is: It has to be your new constant. How can you nurture people, make them better than you, better than they were the day before? Inspiration for me is all about changing people's lives and helping them realise things they thought were impossible. One of the keys to leadership, and to having my team look up to me, is being happy to hire people who are way better than me. I know the people who work for me can walk on water in their field, and I'm okay with that. My job as a leader is only to find them.

So, the constant is also: How can I grow them even further? I've had many technically outstanding team members who could generate mathematical equations I couldn't even begin to understand. But they often lacked senior management speech, presentation, and confidence during senior meetings. My job, then, is to give them that extra nudge. So, in being inspirational, consistency is key. We're not talking about one-off interventions or giving them a new mountain, the size of Everest, for the individual to climb each month. For me, it's about giving them a little pebble every single day, then making that pebble fractionally bigger so they can always stand on top of that pebble and feel amazing about it.

The third step is: Inspiring people doesn't come when times are easy. They come when things are tough, when mistakes have been made. It's during those times that people will look up to you to see what your reaction will be – if you're panicking, if you're stressed, if you're angry. If your reaction can be one of leading and pulling people together, then you're on the right path. How do you develop consistency? If you remember the John and the anti-John, one reason John was so inspirational is that when the crisis hit, his ability to look unfazed was spectacular. His tone of voice was also very calm and unrushed. It was as simple for him to enter (what we call) the War Room as it is for him to meet someone in the street and say, "Good morning, how are you?".

It might sound trivial, but those abilities to deal with uncertainty are what make you inspirational. When things go wrong, it's a natural human instinct to look up, to see who the leader is, and to see how they react. For me, an inspirational leader can create the feeling of safety. If your team feels safe, you'll be fine. Things will move forward in a calm, rational, constructive way. But if the person at the helm seems to panic, things are going to get much worse because people will be seeking their own solutions. Their brain will kick in, saying: "Oh, it's a desperate situation. I need to do something", and no tangible progress will be made. So developing the competency of becoming John, for a better word, is a constant task.

Let's add our fourth step (a question): Do I need to be superhuman? Absolutely not. I've been presented with many situations where the first thing that comes to mind is anger, stress, or other negative emotions. Typically at that time, the team wants to drag you into a meeting you're not prepared for. There's nothing wrong in asking your team to give you a minute. (It doesn't mean give me a whole hour, or that I'm running away from the situation.) One minute gives me more than enough time to compose myself and calm down.

One of my favourite tips is to walk away from the keyboard if your job is keyboard-based. Physically stepping away from the situation has done wonders for my ability to become grounded again. And being grounded helps me stay calm, which in turn signals to the team that I'm in control.

The fifth step is: Remember that being inspirational doesn't make you a preacher. It's also about choosing what you're going to say, when you're going to say it, and where you're going to say it. Inspiration is also about growth, aspiration, and change. It's important to recognise that not everyone will find you inspirational. Remember, this is not adoration – you're not God. And also, not everyone wants to grow.

Part of creating a high-performing team is having the ability to recognise that some of your team members are very happy to do their work and leave, and there's nothing wrong with that. The beauty of high-performance teams is having people who possess different levels of performance. A whole team of high-fliers, as the corporate jargon goes, would be extremely hard for you to manage because they'd all want the next promotion instantly. Remember, not everyone wants to grow at the same speed that you or the company might want.

The final step is: Remember you're not for everyone. In coaching, for example, the coach doesn't have the ability to coach every single client on the planet, because we all have different preferences. It's the same as being inspirational. Not *everyone* will find you inspirational – but if you do a good job, no-one will see you as that dreaded manager who makes people cringe, roll their eyes, and go: "Oh my God, what is this going to be about this time?".

Those six points highlight what it's taken me to become inspirational. And remember, even today as I write this book, whenever someone says to me something like, "Wow, you're inspirational", or "Wow, you changed my life", I still have to pinch myself. It's not something I take for granted. But I think the reason why it still resonates is because it's a validation that I did my job well by helping them. As I said earlier, this isn't adoration. I'm not the God they're praying to. All I do is give them the nudge, give them the push, be by their side when done and when they need someone to help them conquer that obstacle. If you think about it, reaching senior leadership only involves navigating a road strewn with obstacles. We're not talking of an unclimbable mountain. We're talking about a road that isn't always easy – but if it were easy, everyone could do it.

So as an inspirational leader, your job is to be the best coach you can be for your people. Remember, it's great to talk the talk, but it's harder to walk the walk. I'll give you some examples of what I've had the privilege of seeing. I've seen quite a few CEOs who branded themselves inspirational or the best leaders the company's ever seen. (We're talking C-level.) For a few, the modus operandi when they entered the room in a crisis was not to command the room, but to take it over. They clearly thought: "I'm going to take the pen and start blurting out my ideas on the whiteboard for the next thirty minutes, even though the meeting had nothing to do with what I'm saying". Yet although their colleagues might find it funny once, by the third time they're going to start thinking, "Oh my gosh, they just entered the room again".

So, how did being inspirational help me create high-performing teams?

While I got my inspiration from John, it really boils down to doing things differently:

Motivation: For me, a motivated team is a performing team. When people are inspired, they're more likely to be enthusiastic and committed to their work, leading to increased effort and dedication.

Shared Vision: I'm a huge advocate of sharing my vision. Transparency has really helped in creating loyalty and making everyone feel that they're part of a single team. When I communicate my vision with my teams, it helps them create a sense of purpose and direction, aligning everyone with common goals.

Boosted Morale: Inspiration can uplift team morale, even during challenging times. Inspirational leaders can encourage team members to stay positive, persevere, and see setbacks as opportunities for growth. I'm a strong believer in seeing the glass half full rather than half empty. Experience has showed me that it's very hard to come out of a situation when all you see is doom and gloom.

Enhanced Creativity: An inspired team is more likely to think creatively and come up with innovative solutions to problems. Inspiration can foster an environment where team members feel encouraged to share their ideas and take calculated risks. Nothing can help fix a situation like brainstorming, which fosters creativity and helps people feel part of the solution.

Stronger Team Cohesion: Something that really rubs me the wrong way is when teams develop a "them and us" culture where finger-pointing is the first and preferred way of working. Cohesion can enhance communication, collaboration, and trust among team members, which are crucial for high performance.

Resilience: High-performing teams face challenges and setbacks, but resilience can help them bounce back quickly. This is when being part of the team (vs being in an ivory tower) has been shown to boost emotional wellbeing and ensured that the team knows that there *is* a tomorrow and we'll bounce back, no matter how bad the current situation is.

I've also seen people (and C-levels) being extremely harsh on people, which has always made me cringe. This often comes with a wrapping-up sentence along the lines of, "Oh, remember, I'm here for you. I'm here to support you. I'm here to make your life easier, I have your back, I know what you need". The challenge with being inspirational is that if those words become void of meaning, then you've completely lost it. And remember, the corporate world is made up of insanely bright people. No-one's there by accident, especially at senior level. Consequently, people are also very quick to see if inspirational sentiments are true, or if they're just a series of buzzwords.

Small, surprising things can be inspirational. It doesn't have to be that massive mountain that you've helped someone climb, or creating a Pulitzer Prize–winning book. It can be very, very small. It could be as simple as helping the lowest person on the food chain (the coffee boy, for example) and treating them like a human. I promise you, the way you'll appear in their eyes is worth the effort. Being kind can transform someone's life.

The beauty of being inspirational is the phenomenal ripple effect you may create by helping one person. Wrapping up what it takes to be inspirational, if you want other people to think highly of you, yet also want them to think you're always right, no-one will ever look up to you or wish to emulate you.

People follow others because of who they are, not because of their rank or position. Some of the most inspirational leaders have no title. But to finish this chapter, I'd like to quote American author and entrepreneur Tim Fargo: "Leadership is service, not position. Inspirational isn't a title you own, it's something that's given. It's a byproduct. And the irony of being truly inspirational is that you must suspend your ego and serving others gives that".

CHAPTER 9

YOU MADE IT TO EXEC ... NOW WHAT?

ARE YOU READY FOR THE BEST RIDE OF YOUR LIFE?

L et me start with a quote from Mother Teresa, which I think summarises well what executive leadership is all about: "I alone cannot change the world, but I can cast a stone across the water to create many ripples".

This chapter will enable you to understand how executive leadership isn't the sum of individual teams, but an exponential ability to influence, lead, and change lives on a greater scale than you could possibly imagine. Have you ever wondered what makes some teams outperform others each and every time? How some departments have people who'd happily work 24 hours a day whilst others can't wait to leave the workplace and go home one minute past the end of the working day? How come some apparently normal middle-of-the-road managers will be remembered years and sometimes decades after they've left? How do some of those managers have such a profound effect on the people they managed, while others leave them with scars that will never heal? The answer isn't money. Go figure. What makes those people so special, so different that they have a profound effect on the whole organisation they manage?

Having managed people for thirty years, I'd been an exec for well over ten years by the time I started writing this book. It really can come down to five different steps. And for that I'm going to use a comparison, which hopefully you can follow. Running an organisation is a bit like being the trunk of a tree. If the trunk doesn't do its job, the leaves won't flourish. The first step to being a successful executive is to make sure your tree has the right branches. Very often, it's impossible to choose a direct report and we inherit a team. How can we help those one level down – our big branches, the ones that are really attached to the trunk – to follow the right frame of mind and help them understand that their actions will ultimately impact the smaller branches and leaves?

One of the key characteristics of the trunk and branches is to be visible. Visibility, especially during hard times, is what put people's minds at rest. People need stability. Being consistently visible instils stability. For example, I love walking the floor daily, even if it's just to say, "Good morning" – there's nothing better than for my people to see me. And believe me, this isn't about ego. In one of my jobs, I noticed that after I came back from a holiday, people immediately came to see me; it was simply the lack of stability they had when I wasn't there. So, as a trunk of the tree, your people need you. If you follow that tree metaphor, the nutrients from the ground can only reach the branches (and ultimately the leaves) if they go through the trunk.

So be visible, walk the floor, talk to people. If you do one-to-ones, *keep* those one-to-ones. If you can only afford to do them on a biweekly basis because your agenda is busy, stick to that schedule; don't do them for two weeks and then stop doing them. Visibility and stability create corporate safety. When people feel safe, they can stop focusing on themselves and wondering whether their job – and by extension, their family – is safe. They can then get back to serving the company.

Talk, talk, and talk more; people love to feel valued. For example, I'd never have thought that something as simple as a "Good morning" or "Well done" or "That was great" would have this much impact. Even a "Thank you" can have a profound effect on someone. I remember many times where something didn't go well, and I was working really closely with one of my direct reports and we fixed the problem. Well, to be fair, the ownership of fixing and the ability to fix it was more on them than me. I just acted as their sounding board. By the end of it, when everything was fine again, saying something as simple as "Thank you for all you did" completely changed a person's physiology. Even though we'd been under stress for hours, instantly they relaxed and smiled and really felt like they were worth a million dollars – which to be fair, they are to me; I can't do anything without my people.

No-one can perform at any level unless they feel safe. People need to know that work is a safe place where they won't get abused, and where their mental health will be preserved. This is one of the key factors of what will make you an outstanding executive. How much can you create that feeling of safety and enabling workers to know that they'll leave work at the end of the day with good mental health, allowing them to focus on their family and friends?

Psychological safety at work is not just nice to have, but a duty of every single exec to create. And this can be done by establishing a deep relationship between the different levels of the organisation. Throughout my career, my direct reports knew that they would never be abused or shouted at. And no matter what they told me, even if I didn't like it, I wouldn't make it about them. I've had people coming to tell me, "I've destroyed the production system. We're losing money", or "My team made a mistake, and this is now completely broken". Whatever the example, you name it, I've had it. An article by Camille Preston in *Psychology Today* explains that creating psychological safety at works goes way beyond people feeling safe. It demonstrates how safety is a cornerstone of creating high-performing teams. I've outlined some of Camille's main points about psychological safety below.

Safety serves as an engine for performance: Because psychological safety encourages risk-taking, which is connected to both creativity and innovation, some researchers characterise psychological safety as an "engine for performance". If you think about it, your teams will be much more inclined to think outside the box and push themselves when they know there won't be any negative repercussions of making a mistake.

Encourage candid feedback: We know that candid feedback is vital and that it can be difficult to share honest and actionable feedback in a low-trust environment. High levels of psychological safety help build workplaces where feedback can be easily shared on an ongoing basis, driving better outcomes. In my opinion, feedback is the key element of growth, highlighting potential blind spots and allowing you to act on them.

Help team members with lower confidence speak up: One of the most important impacts of psychological safety is its ability to help team members with lower confidence be heard.

Increase retention: For the above reasons, high levels of psychological safety are also strongly correlated with increased retention. In the current job market, where finding and retaining talent is a growing challenge, investing in psychological safety offers a clear return for teams and organisations. In my opinion, a characteristic of low-performing organisations is a tendency to see people as numbers (or as I've heard once, "disposable assets"). Increasing retention doesn't just reduce hiring costs; it also reduces loss of corporate knowledge/know-how, potential customer relationships, and so much more.

The flip side is without safety, people won't raise their concerns.

Why Employees Are Reluctant to Use Their Voices

They know that speaking up at work mainly benefits the organization, not the individual employee.

	Who benefits	When benefit occurs	Certainty of benefit
Voice	The organization and/or its customers	After some delay	Low
Silence	Oneself	Immediately	High

Source: Adapted from *The Fearless Organization,* by Amy C. Edmondson (Wiley, 2018) ▽**HBR**

The above *Harvard Business Review* (HBR) study shows the effect on the organisation when employees feel empowered to speak, compared to when they prefer not speaking up.

The ability to stay focused also helps the organisation grow. Again, if we focus back on the tree, if the main branch attached to the trunk doesn't feel valued and safe, the smaller branches and leaves won't feel safe either. Just like the nutrients flowing from the trunk to the leaves, good news or bad news gets passed down that same tree extremely quickly.

One of the key differences between being an executive and being a manager or head of department is that your job is to grow leaders, not managers. One of the jobs as a next step is to help your successor leave the biggest and most positive impact on the organisation. If you think about it, executive-level jobs, as well as helping a company flourish (and I'm not saying that growth of people has to be to the detriment of the company's vision and day-to-day business), are about growing *leaders*, not managers. How can you go the extra mile to start creating your own legacy in the company? How can you grow your successors so when you're on holiday, the world is fine? *Harvard Business Review* demonstrates the key difference between managers and people leaders.

From Manager to People Leader

Three fundamental shifts in the role of managers today

A power shift: from "me" to "we"		
My team makes me successful.	→	I'm here to make my team successful.
I'm rewarded for achieving business goals.	→	I'm also rewarded for improving team engagement, inclusion, and skills relevancy.
I control how people move beyond my unit.	→	I scout for talent and help my team move fluidly to wider opportunities.

A skills shift: from task overseer to performance coach		
I oversee work.	→	I track outcomes.
I assess team members against expectations.	→	I coach them to achieve their potential and invite their feedback on my management.
I provide work direction and share information from above.	→	I supply inspiration, sensemaking, and emotional support.

A structural shift: from static and physical to fluid and digital		
I manage an intact team of people in fixed jobs in a physical workplace.	$\longrightarrow$	My team is fluid, and the workplace is digital.
I set goals and make assessments annually.	$\longrightarrow$	I provide ongoing guidance on priorities and performance feedback.
I hold an annual career discussion focused on the next promotion.	$\longrightarrow$	I'm always retraining my team and providing career coaching.

▽ HBR

This highlights that a traditional manager who's "me" focused is less focused on developing the organisation they belong to. The immediate result is a team who will grow less, be less independent, and feel more constrained in task execution. Yet this is also a very short-sighted approach. Without growth, there's no succession planning for that leader, which also means no promotion.

Remember, your branches can only be nourished by what you feed them. If you feed your staff a leadership style that's based on being autocratic, demeaning and abusive, that's what they'll feed people below them. At that point, a whole part of the tree could be dwindling down while another is growing, depending on your leadership style. Let's look at what social psychology says about leadership styles and how this can impact a team's performance: Is there any evidence of a correlation between style and performance, and is there any difference in team behaviour when a leader of each style is present or not?

A study by Kurt Lewin (often referred to as the founder of social psychology) and colleagues demonstrated the impact of autocratic leadership style on people and their behaviour. They experimentally created three "social climates"— authoritarian, democratic, and laissez-faire. To create these, an adult would act in accordance with one style while leading a group of ten-year-old boys. To be **authoritarian**, the leader would determine all the policies of the group and dictate the work task; to be **democratic**, the leader would encourage group discussion about policies and facilitate group decision-making; and **laissez-faire** leadership allowed complete freedom for the group with little or no participation from the leader. Accordingly, a laissez-faire style of leadership was deemed so ineffective for group functioning that it was abandoned in future studies as a leadership style.

In Lewin's studies, they found that when leaders were present, performance was roughly equal between the autocratic and democratic groups, but when the leaders left, performance declined for those in the autocratic group but not for the democratic group. They also found, as one might guess, more submission of group members to authoritarian leaders and a greater need for instruction and directions.

They also observed more hostility in the autocratic group compared to the democratic group, most notably when the leader was absent. Among many factors, Lewin and colleagues surmised this was a result of the "tension" created in the group (what we might now call "stress"), and that this tension needed an outlet, which was through hostility. While Lewin and colleagues were interested in how leadership styles promoted aggression, one might conclude that a more hostile environment with more submission is not a climate where individuals will freely speak their minds.

As demonstrated above, there is clear evidence that style greatly impacts team performance. It also shows that empowering teams allows performance to remain stable even when the leader isn't present.

One other thing that comes with leadership and executive level is exhaustion, as the demands of running a department and the weight of responsibility isn't negligible. Experience has showed me that it isn't the responsibilities themselves that make leadership more challenging; it's the impact of every decision and the ripple effect each one has. Leadership requires ensuring that all the company policies are respected to guarantee as much as possible that the employees' and the company's interests are protected. A simple signature or email approval no longer impacts one person. It impacts a team, a whole department, or potentially the whole company. In addition, execs carry the burden of past decisions made even before they were in charge and have to deal with the consequences of those, whether good or bad. I tried once to explain a bad situation by saying "It was before my time", and the response was swift and very unpleasant. What struck me is that there's no decision that one can't own as an exec, be it past, present or future. There's no such thing as a "decision expiry date" that would allow the exec to have an easy exit. This is the "weight of responsibilities". However, it's not all doom and gloom …

Based on my experience, from this point onwards, it's a good idea to have a **coach**, a **mentor**, or someone external to talk to, because a problem shared is a problem halved. I can recall many times where I was faced with huge decisions and had no-one to talk to and the detrimental effect that had on me, which we'll cover in the next chapter on burnout. The people I'm fortunate enough to coach can and do share their stories with me, which helps them recall who they truly are. It makes sure, in our tree example, that the trunk is healthy. It helps them make sure that what they give to their branches is the best of themselves. I was fortunate to have great mentors. One situation when mentorship helped me was after about ten years in my career, when a colleague (and friend) and I were asked to step up to replace an executive who'd just left. The job was much too big for either of us at that point of our lives, and we were asked to split the role as we both saw fit. (We were talking an equivalent of ten technology departments to manage.) This is when my mentor was invaluable and truly helped me understand that splitting the job was a good idea, as it would allow both of us to show our strengths; it would also make it manageable as we were moving from managing one team to overseeing five, which required a whole new skillset. Jerry, my mentor, didn't reveal that they lacked faith in my ability to manage ten teams. Instead, he helped me understand what it meant to manage multiple teams and how to go about it. As Jerry was also in the company, his mentoring gave me truly invaluable insights not only on the new job, but the expectations and landscape I was moving into in terms of corporate politics and powers at play.

One of the things that comes with being an executive, no matter the level of the organisation beneath you, is that others will look up to you for an answer. No matter the situation, no matter the problem, you'll be expected to have all the answers instantly (or at least rapidly). This is why mentorship, coaching, or both can have a hugely beneficial effect on you as a leader. It will halve the burden of running the company, while allowing you to preserve your mental health by having the opportunity to vent.

We spoke about preserving the team's mental health. What do you do to keep yours checked? How do you ensure that you're not mentally exhausted before having even left the bed? If we were to summarise what being an executive is, always remember that your organisation is only as strong as your weakest link. (This is *not* an open invitation to find the weakest link.) Also, an organisation with only high performance is totally unmanageable. Whilst numbers, KPIs, and balance sheets are important, remember that, as the trunk of the tree, you must help your branches to coach your weakest link.

One of the things I've done multiple times in the past, which helps me check the health of my organisation and the people in it, is to call what are termed skip-level meetings. Very regularly, I'll ask my second line of reports to have a one-to-one with me. First, this allows me to assess how my directs are performing. Second, it allows me to start understanding a bit better the people who work for me, with whom I wouldn't necessarily interact every day. It also allows me to start gauging who's a potential future leader, because in those conversations I can start to understand and appreciate the person, their work, their style, and all the things that make them who they are.

The beauty of those skip meetings and 360-degree performance reviews is having two-way feedback. It could be that I have a blind spot (and I'm sure I do), so I'll ask those people what I can do to also improve myself. Many times in the past, I've used those skip-level meetings to understand how the flow of information trickles down the organisation, what's on my team's mind, and what's worrying them. During one of those skip-level meetings, I learned that running quarterly town halls didn't meet my team's expectations; there was a need for meetings with smaller audiences, as it would help my team feel more open to ask me questions. Another great outcome of those skip-level meetings is that they also gave me feedback on my direct reports, helping me remove any biases I might have. Executive level isn't just about balance sheets or people; it's a combination of both.

If I had to draw one conclusion – which many companies forget at times – no matter what the company sells or how profitable it is, it's worth remembering that without its people, the company doesn't exist. I don't know a single company where the assets aren't its people. Even if it's heavily reliant on machinery, you still need people to operate that company. You need people to make each decision. So, as an exec, how can you be the strongest trunk you possibly can be to ensure all the nutrients in the ground are passed to your branches, so they can then pass them onto *their* branches and finally to the leaves?

CHAPTER 10

BURNOUT ...
WHAT DID IT TEACH ME?

*HOW LONG WOULD IT TAKE WHEN YOU LEAVE
YOUR JOB BEFORE THE COMPANY MOVES ON?*

Ariana Huffington, founder of *The Huffington Post*, allegedly said: "The land of burnout is not a place I ever want to go back to".

By the end of this chapter, I hope you can recognise the signs of burnout before it hits you and find some of the tricks I've used to both learn from it and prevent it happening again.

As an article in *Harvard Business Review* says:

*"EMPLOYEE BURNOUT IS A COMMON
PHENOMENON, BUT IT IS ONE THAT COMPANIES
TEND TO TREAT AS A TALENT MANAGEMENT
OR PERSONAL ISSUE RATHER THAN A BROADER
ORGANISATIONAL CHALLENGE. THAT'S A MISTAKE.*

*"THE PSYCHOLOGICAL AND PHYSICAL PROBLEMS
OF BURNED-OUT EMPLOYEES, WHICH COST*

AN ESTIMATED $125 BILLION TO $190 BILLION A YEAR IN HEALTHCARE SPENDING IN THE U.S., ARE JUST THE MOST OBVIOUS IMPACTS. THE TRUE COST TO BUSINESS CAN BE FAR GREATER, THANKS TO LOW PRODUCTIVITY ACROSS ORGANIZATIONS, HIGH TURNOVER, AND THE LOSS OF THE MOST CAPABLE TALENT."

For me, burnout is not like being hit by a ton of bricks. It's not being so tired that you want to fall in a heap. It's sneaky. It creeps upon you. It lingers and waits to see what you'll do about looking after yourself. Many times, I've started a new job and wanted to prove myself. And whilst going the extra mile can be rewarding, I failed to notice the physical impact of constantly working.

It started by me becoming tired earlier than usual during the day, needing my sleep more than usual at the weekend, and not being able to go for a workout because sleep is more important. And before I knew it, my brain goes on standard mode near-permanently.

I wanted to share with you some of those things that worked for me, and also some that didn't. One of the first things to recognise is that many companies love "hero syndrome" the notion that working every hour of the day is amazing. The culture makes you feel that the longer you work, the less food you can eat, the better you are, and the more you'll be rewarded. That's a hero syndrome, but it's also one of the best ways to become burned out.

One of the things I didn't have at the beginning, but helped me a lot once I got it, was having someone to talk to. It can be a mentor; it can be a coach. A coach may recommend a therapist, or perhaps you can find one yourself, or a partner with whom you can share what's on your mind and how it's affecting you. This will not only help you clear your mind, but also give you a totally different perspective on the situation.

Meditation is one of the things that worked for me. I want to dissipate a myth of what meditation is or isn't for me. Meditation for me doesn't mean staying perfectly still for hours on end, thinking of nothing. This is totally unrealistic, and has the potential to wind you up badly. I remember the first time I tried meditation. It was with an app, and I thought it said to sit down and empty my brain for fifteen minutes and think of nothing. But it didn't work for me at that stage; I hadn't trained my brain, and it didn't know how to do nothing for fifteen minutes. It's been a long journey to get where I am with meditation now; for me, the trick was to start with thirty seconds, then build up to fifteen minutes. One other thing I've noticed is that our brain can't think about nothing. It's close to impossible.

Something else that works for me, however, is to focus on one really pleasant thought. It could be nature, it could be your breath, it could be anything; come back to it whenever you feel yourself drifting away. To help me with this, I've used apps that got me started within fifteen seconds. What also encouraged me to stick to it is to have someone holding me accountable. And my biggest challenge is exactly that. I'll regularly meditate in the morning, which helps me get in a great place. Then, I give it up because I'm in a great place, instead of realising that it's exactly what helped me.

I'm not, and never will be, a Buddhist monk who can do nothing for a whole day. Mediation's a step-by-step process, and I don't believe the books should tell you what you should or shouldn't do. It's truly whatever works for you. Some people like it with music, others like it completely quiet. The reason why I mentioned that is ages ago, I heard a quote about Usain Bolt that made me smile and was applicable here: "When Usain Bolt goes to buy something in the corner shop, he doesn't do it sprinting". And by that, I mean that you don't have to be the best runner all the time; taking it easy is important too.

Another tip that worked well for me is walking. I'm not blessed with a Greek god's body, so I can't tell you I go to the gym and work out fifteen times a week. Although this is one of the first things I gave up in some of my jobs, walking has worked really well. My wife has introduced me to something as simple as a morning walk. It doesn't have to be brisk; it doesn't have to be speedy; and it doesn't have to make me sweat, but going out has proven to do me the world of good.

Being indoors most of the day also takes a tonne of the vitamin D your body produces, but it needs direct sunlight hitting your skin to produce it. (And no, a computer screen with a blue filter doesn't count.) As I said, walking makes me go out. I believe it doesn't have to be a walk, just something that's completely different from your daily routine. So if you're a desk worker, what can you do to be more physically active without using your brain? And again, I don't profess to be a personal trainer or train endlessly so that I look like Dwayne Johnson – far from it.

Helping someone else just for the fun of it is a great help. When I help others by coaching or volunteering, it gives me a great sense of purpose and achievement; it also helps my brain release dopamine and put things in perspective. One of the reasons behind that is when you're super active, in a high-powered position with responsibility, it's very easy to focus on yourself and say, "What can I do to be more productive faster? Help the people at work, deliver my numbers ...?". Because with senior positions come senior responsibility. And really what you need to do, instead of focusing on yourself, is focus on something that gives you satisfaction, whatever it is. It can be helping others, or doing art. I know lots of people who took up painting to trigger the creative part of their brain while giving the logical part of their brain a rest, helping them relax.

The final tip is to do something social. If you think about it, the higher you go up the corporate food chain, the lonelier it is. You're expected to become bigger and bigger and bigger, everyone looks up to you, you have numbers to deliver or costs to reduce ... whatever it is. Doing something social allows you to be in contact with people again, providing that feeling of belonging to a bigger community. For some people, it's football; for others it's paddling, tennis, squash, or golf – wherever works for you.

Creating this little social bubble with your friends also allows you to rant. Trust me, there's nothing wrong in expressing to a good friend from time to time how you feel about work, pressure, whatever it may be. But it will also allow you to have another perspective on who you are and the challenges you're facing. Also, you'll get that nice comforting feeling that you're not on your own.

I hope those tips have helped a bit. Now, I'd like to share a story of when I *really* hit burnout. For the sake of anonymity, we're going to say I work for a hotel, though the real company is in a different sector. Let's say I took over the whole hotel as COO, then had to turn that company around and make it hit numbers that were much bigger than the current trend. As the COO, you normally have a CEO and a structure around you to help you run the company. In this case, there was no structure around. From Day One, it was virtually "Here you go – run the company, go figure it out". As you can imagine, I faced two challenges immediately. One was that I'd been parachuted into a company I knew nothing about, with a culture I knew nothing about, and with an extremely tight deadline to turn it around – and so my challenge was to find my feet as quickly as possible. The second was that the company is in an industry I had no experience in – so on top of learning the structure and culture of the company, I had to master a new industry as quickly as possible.

After checking attrition and all the usual indicators, I realised that the company's existing culture – such as an autocratic decision-making process and very different values between the top and the bottom – was one of the reasons it was facing so many challenges. As COO, I quickly had to become the buffer between the people. My job was to make sure people didn't leave, because they're the company's biggest asset. While I was working and doing a great job of taking the business to a better place, I was taking on negative energy and saying, "Well, how can I make sure my people are fine without having the previous behaviour continuing, then change them really quickly?".

As time went by, I started finding myself more and more tight; I couldn't figure out what was going on, because the company was turning around really well, attrition went down, and the numbers started to go up. On paper, everything should have been great. After a while, some of the senior management behaviour really started rubbing me the wrong way. In retrospect, I realised that it contradicted my deepest values, traits, and beliefs. I was in constant conflict with myself, while still trying to turn the company around.

One of my traits, as you know, is being very introverted. And let's say my manager was very extroverted and a loud shouter. Whilst the people under me loved it because I wasn't shouting at them, I was being, for example, shouted at.

This very slowly chipped away at who I am, because I was taking something that doesn't resonate with me. While the company was turning around, it was at my personal cost, which was very expensive. The thing that made me realise the cost was too great was when I'd come home, I couldn't watch TV with my wife. We could barely have a conversation because by nine o'clock in the evening, without me realising it, I'd fall asleep. It also caused me to cancel all my good habits, which I spoke about earlier – I wouldn't go to the gym, play golf, go for walks, or meditate anymore. Instead, I'd focused everything I had on turning the company around.

So. how do I make sure my teams don't burn out?

Studies show that, when looking at companies with high burnout rates, three common culprits were present: excessive collaboration, weak time management, and a tendency to overload the most capable with too much work. These forces not only rob employees of time to concentrate on completing complex tasks and generating ideas, but also crunch the downtime that's necessary for restoration. What does this mean practically, and what can be done about it?

Excessive collaboration leads to endless meetings, emails, and multitasking, causing overloading of work schedules and burnout. To address this issue, companies can streamline their organisational structures, assess the necessity of meetings, and assemble high-energy, high-achieving teams for critical tasks. Promoting a culture of respecting employees' time can also help mitigate burnout.

Weak time-management practices are prevalent in large organisations, where collaboration demands have outpaced effective tools and norms. Executives often overlook the costs of excessive collaboration. Workplace tools like Microsoft Workplace Analytics can help organisations measure and manage employee time usage effectively. Identifying areas where time is wasted in meetings, emails, and online collaboration can lead to targeted changes and increased productivity. Empowering employees with control over their calendars and avoiding micromanagement can also reduce stress. After all, time is the only resource we'll never have enough of, and the only one money can't buy.

Overloading the most capable employees is a common issue, especially when hiring doesn't match growth. Highly talented managers often bear the brunt of collaboration overload, impacting their productivity. Workplace analytics tools can help assess the excess demands on top managers' time, enabling adjustments to workflows and workload distribution.

To combat burnout, leaders must change organisational norms and prioritise giving employees the time needed to focus on critical tasks. This approach can lead to increased productivity, reduced burnout, and improved overall wellbeing for employees.

The moral of my story is that there has to be a balance. As a result, I made myself a promise: Never will I sacrifice all of who I am, and all of my little habits that keep me sane, for the benefit of any company. Because if you think about it, how long does it take for the company to move on after you've left? If you're someone who's critical to the company, it might be a month, but it's never going to be a lifetime. Compare that to how long it would take for your husband or wife to recover if you completely burn out and need to rest for three months.

I wish I could say it's easy to look after yourself religiously every day, but that would be a lie. What I would say is don't beat yourself up. If one day you feel like not doing self-care, that's okay, but try to be consistent. Also, when everything feels great, that might be when you're tempted to skip it. What does great feel like? How can you tell when everything has changed?

Juliet Obodo, a hypnotherapist, said burnout exists because we made rest a reward rather than a right. What my experience told me is that more and more big corporates expect the hero syndrome of overwork. And I've witnessed companies being shocked by employees leaving because they can't have time to themselves at the weekend, and managers challenging their employees to earn rest.

CONCLUSION

Congratulations on completing the book! As Clare – my amazing book coach – would tell me when I completed milestones in writing this book, "Go and reward yourself". I hope this book has created some different emotions ranging from laughter, to "aha" moments, to disbelief that some management practices still exist.

As we conclude this journey through the corridors of corporate leadership, I hope you've discovered that the summit needn't be a lonely place. In writing *How Not to Be Lonely at the Top: Practical Wisdom for Positive Corporate Leadership and High-Performing Teams*, my aim was to equip you with the tools, strategies, and insights to navigate the challenges and triumphs of leadership with a renewed sense of purpose and connection.

From the first chapter to the last, we've explored real-world situations that corporate leaders often encounter, and I've shared my three decades of experience to illuminate the path forward.

Remember, loneliness at the top is a choice. By applying the practical wisdom within these pages, you can build enduring relationships, foster trust, and create a supportive community that ensures your leadership journey remains fulfilling and far from solitary. The summit is yours to conquer, and with the lessons learned here, you can thrive at the top, embracing the camaraderie and companionship that comes with effective leadership.

By now, you've become the Master Chef and you deserve to be equipped with all the different recipes of life, tips and tricks about leading, managing people, and creating high-performing teams. Remember that Michelin-starred chefs don't cook on their own; they have a whole set of skilled people around them. This doesn't have to be the end of our journey, and I'm here for you if you wish.

Let's get connected!

If this book resonated with you and you want to have someone who won't judge but can act as a sounding board on your journey, please reach out to me. Email me on philippe@philippemathijs.com or check my website at www.philippemathijs.com. Additionally, scan the QR code below for bonus goodies ... just because you're amazing!

Remember you're great, and we *all* have the ability to be outstanding.

Philippe Mathijs

Executive and Leadership Coach and Advisor

HOW ARE YOU WIRED? QUESTIONNAIRE

P lease answer the following questions honestly and choose the option that best describes you.

1. When solving problems or making decisions, I'm most likely to:
    a) rely on logic, facts, and data.
    b) trust my intuition and gut feelings.
    c) consider how my decisions will impact others emotionally.
    d) seek creative and innovative solutions.

2. In a group discussion or meeting, I tend to:
    a) focus on analysing and organising information.
    b) listen to my instincts and feelings about the topic.
    c) pay attention to the emotions and dynamics of the group.
    d) generate new ideas and think outside the box.

3. When learning something new, I prefer:
    a) a structured and organised approach with clear steps.
    b) exploring and experimenting on my own.

c)   collaborating with others and discussing the topic.

d)   engaging in creative and imaginative activities.

4.   My decision-making style is best described as:
a)   systematic and methodical.
b)   trusting my instincts and following my heart.
c)   Considerate of how others will be affected emotionally.
d)   open to exploring novel and unconventional options.

5.   In my free time, I enjoy activities that involve:
a)   solving puzzles, analysing data, or reading.
b)   connecting with nature, meditation, or artistic pursuits.
c)   spending time with friends, talking, or empathising.
d)   creating art, brainstorming, or trying new experiences.

6.   When faced with a challenge, my initial response is to:
a)   gather information and assess the situation.
b)   listen to my instincts and trust my feelings.
c)   consider the feelings and needs of those involved.
d)   brainstorm creative solutions and explore possibilities.

7.   I feel most fulfilled when I:
a)   achieve clear and measurable goals.
b)   follow my passions and intuition.
c)   help others and create harmonious relationships.
d)   innovate, create, and push boundaries.

8. My preferred mode of communication is:
   a) logical and well-structured.
   b) intuitive and emotionally expressive.
   c) compassionate and empathetic.
   d) imaginative and visionary.

Scoring:

- Count the number of times you selected each letter (a, b, c, d).
- The letter with the highest count represents your preferred brain quadrant.

Results:

- If you have mostly 'a' answers, your preferred quadrant might be the "CEO brain" quadrant.
- If you have mostly 'b' answers, your preferred quadrant might be the "so what" quadrant.
- If you have mostly 'c' answers, your preferred quadrant might be the "COO brain" quadrant.
- If you have mostly 'd' answers, your preferred quadrant might be the "Board brain" quadrant.

WHAT ARE YOUR TRAITS, VALUES AND BEHAVIOURS?

Instructions

Answer the following questions honestly. After completing all the questions, we'll help you identify your top three traits, values, and behaviours.

Traits

For each of the following statements, rate how well it describes you on a scale of 1 to 5, with 1 being "Not at all" and 5 being "Very much".

1. I enjoy socialising and meeting new people.
    [ ] 1
    [ ] 2
    [ ] 3
    [ ] 4
    [ ] 5

2. I tend to be organised and structured in my daily life.
    [ ] 1
    [ ] 2
    [ ] 3
    [ ] 4
    [ ] 5

3. I'm open to trying new and adventurous experiences.
    [ ] 1
    [ ] 2
    [ ] 3
    [ ] 4
    [ ] 5

Values

For each of the following values, rank them in order of importance to you, with 1 being the most important and 5 being the least important.
    [ ] Family
    [ ] Career success
    [ ] Honesty
    [ ] Environmental sustainability
    [ ] Freedom

Behaviours

Think about how you typically behave in certain situations and select the option that best represents you.

1. In a conflict with a friend or colleague, I'm most likely to:
    [ ] Seek compromise and find a solution.
    [ ] Stand my ground and defend my position.
    [ ] Avoid confrontation and let it go.

2. When faced with a challenging task, I tend to:
    [ ] Break it down into manageable steps.
    [ ] Dive in and tackle it head-on.
    [ ] Procrastinate or seek help from others.

3. In social gatherings, I am usually:
    [ ] The life of the party, interacting with everyone.
    [ ] Engaged in deep conversations with a few people.
    [ ] Quiet and observant, taking everything in.

Scoring

Calculate your scores for each category (Traits, Values, Behaviours) and identify your top three in each. Your top three are the traits, values, and behaviours that received the highest scores.

This simple questionnaire/activity can help individuals gain some clarity on their personality traits, core values, and common behaviours. It's important to note that these are just self-assessments and may not encompass the entirety of one's personality or values, but they can be a helpful starting point for self-reflection and personal growth.

Answer the following questions honestly to discover your top three decision-making styles or preferences. Your decision-making styles influence how you approach and make choices in various aspects of your life.

Decision-Making Styles

For each of the following scenarios, select the option that best describes your typical approach to decision-making.

1. When making important life decisions, I tend to:
   [ ] Carefully weigh all pros and cons before deciding.
   [ ] Trust my instincts and make decisions quickly.
   [ ] Seek input and advice from others before deciding.

2. In a group decision-making setting, I usually:
   [ ] Advocate for my own ideas and opinions.
   [ ] Act as a mediator and help the group reach consensus.
   [ ] Prefer to follow the group consensus without much input.

3. When faced with a challenging problem, I am more likely to:
   [ ] Analyse the problem logically and systematically.
   [ ] Rely on creative thinking and innovation.
   [ ] Collaborate with others to find a solution.

Scoring

Calculate your scores for each decision-making style (Analytical, Intuitive, Collaborative) based on your responses. Your top three decision-making styles are the ones you selected most frequently.

Analytical: You tend to make decisions through careful analysis and consideration of facts and data.

Intuitive: You rely on your gut feelings and instincts when making decisions, often opting for quick, intuitive choices.

Collaborative: You value the input and perspectives of others and often involve them in the decision-making process.

Understanding your preferred decision-making styles can help you make more informed choices and adapt your decision-making approach to different situations. Remember that while people may use a combination of these styles depending on the context, identifying your top three can provide valuable insights into your decision-making tendencies.

REFERENCES

The In8model: The easy way to play the game of life by Dr Mark Postles

Coaching definition:

https://www.psychologytoday.com/gb/therapy-types/coaching#:~:text=Psychological%20coaching%20is%20a%20process,be%20interfering%20with%20their%20success.

Loyalty, Wharton Business School:

https://knowledge.wharton.upenn.edu/article/declining-employee-loyalty-a-casualty-of-the-new-workplace/

Psychological safety at work:

https://www.psychologytoday.com/us/blog/mental-health-in-the-workplace/202111/psychological-safety-work

Employee burnout:

https://hbr.org/2017/04/employee-burnout-is-a-problem-with-the-company-not-the-person

BIO

With nearly three decades of corporate experience at international level and the last ten years spent at C-level leadership, Philippe marries hands-on experience of running companies with thousands of hours coaching team leaders and, above all, helping people reach their full potential. He's someone who's been there, with the scars to show it. The constant thread running through Phillipe's career and life is his passion for people and drive to leave a positive legacy to the people, teams, and companies he's served both as a coach and as an executive. Philippe believes people can achieve their desires and aspirations while exploring their potential in a way that will discover new ways of living, operating, behaving, and being. He's truly passionate about seeing people grow and thrive in ways that they deeply desire. He's had the privilege of working with some of the biggest names in business and has received multiple awards, both in coaching and for his leadership in the financial services world.

Philippe's a coach who's operated at executive levels, faced off with the boards of companies, dealt with fundamental business change, and transformed companies. He's a coach who understands the business landscape and your life setting.

EXTRAS

What you need to know about me:

- ✅ Choose from my trio of services: leadership coaching, advisory, and speaking

- ✅ Expertise in business, risk, and IT disciplines

- ✅ Extensive background working with leaders in today's challenging world

- ✅ Dedicated to empowering leaders to be their best selves and achieve outstanding results

- ✅ Founder of Reach Outstanding Business and Leadership coaching school

- ✅ Volunteer coach for organisations including The Hunger Project and Global Shapers Community

My approach is centred around you and your aspirations.

I believe in the power of people and see the possibilities in everyone.

By choosing each other, I'll help you discover better ways of being, behaving, and living – both personally and professionally.

If you're looking to ignite that burning desire within you to achieve more, let's connect on philippe@philippemathijs.com

In addition, as a thank you for reading the book, click on the QR code below to explore some of the free goodies I've created for you.

NOTES

www.ingramcontent.com/pod-product-compliance
Lightning Source LLC
Chambersburg PA
CBHW031858200326
41597CB00012B/466